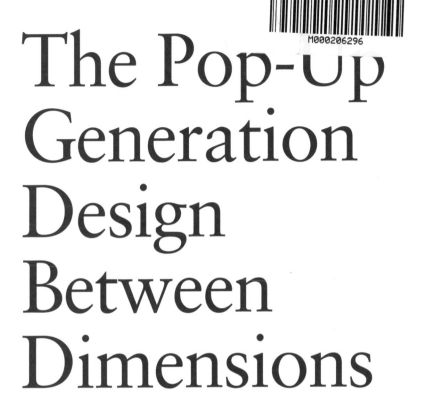

The Pop-Up Generation Design Between Dimensions

ISBN 978-90-6369-282-7

Copyright © 2012 BIS Publishers, MOTI & Edelkoort Exhibitions

Second printing 2013

All images are copyrighted to their respective owners

Many thanks for the generous collaboration of all artists and designers involved in this project.

Thanks to: Michelle Barrios, Clare Butcher, María José García Bravo, Dennis Elbers, Leo Garcia, Caspar van Gemund, Charlotte Hallberg, Merel Noorlander, Bahram Sadeghi, Carolyn Strauss, Jos Tendijck.

mudac MUSÉE DE DESIGN ET D'ARTS APPLIQUÉS CONTEMPORAINS

EDELKOORT EXHIBITIONS

The Pop-Up Generation Design Between Dimensions

Lidewij Edelkoort

MOTI

Commissioned By: MOTI, Museum of the Image, Breda,
                      the Netherlands & mudac, Musée de design et
                      d'arts appliqués contemporains, Lausanne,
                      Switzerland

Concept: Lidewij Edelkoort

Lead Editor: Lotte van Gelder

Design: James Victore, New York
                      Chris Thompson, New York

Editorial Board: Lidewij Edelkoort, Philip Fimmano,
                      Lotte van Gelder, Mieke Gerritzen,
                      Chantal Prod'Hom

Image Research: Lotte van Gelder

Additional
Image Research: Fem Verbeek, Xue Jing Lim

Copy Editor: Akke Pinkster

Texts: Paola Antonelli, Lidewij Edelkoort,
                      Ahmed El Hady, Hedwig Heinsman,
                      Carla Fernández, Lotte van Gelder,
                      Martine Naillon, Bruce Sterling

Production: MOTI, Museum of the Image

Publisher: BIS Publishers, Amsterdam
                      Het Sieraad
                      Postjesweg 1
                      1057 DT Amsterdam
                      The Netherlands
                      T +31 20 515 02 30, F +31 20 515 02 39
                      bis@bispublishers.nl, www.bispublishers.nl

TABLE OF CONTENTS

THE BORDER AREA
By Mieke Gerritzen and Chantal Prod'hom

The new generation of image creators born
at the end of the previous century were just
starting to enjoy an analogue education and
upbringing before being swept away by media
consumption and technological development.
It is a generation more aware of the radical
changes that the digital revolution has unleashed
in society than the generation of those born
after the year 2000.

In this book, we present work by what
we call the Pop-Up Generation; work on the
cusp of design disciplines that stimulates a type
of cultural consciousness and inspires reflection.
Work featuring characteristics of the pop-up
philosophy: temporary, mobile and recyclable.

For creators from this generation, the
ongoing and barely discernible shift from the
second to the third dimension echoes daily life.
The screen provides the viewer with simulated

volumes; often, these are then physically materialized and, immediately thereupon, spread to viewers in the form of new digital input. The two realities, analogue and virtual, engage in unrestricted dialogue. The one never replaces the other, and to surf within the gray zones, where one world blends into another or vice versa, is altogether natural. Today's designers have completely incorporated this practice of to-ing and fro-ing. To them, fleeting fluidity and temporality represent powerfully promising tools: their outlook is conveyed in a spectacular fashion by the wide range of works featured in this publication.

On the one hand, globalization influences the quality of our cultural production; concepts and aesthetic values are influenced by worldwide trends in art and design, as the media illustrates daily. On the other hand, new needs to discover local characteristics rooted in old crafts and specialized knowledge are cropping up. Our renewed interest in traditional approaches, in hand-made craftwork and in the tactile dimension sought through objects reminds us of our need for an identity, implying our belonging to a place and culture to which we can always return.

The boundaries between art and culture are blurring, but so too are those between culture and economy. Whether it is design that is suspended between marketing and management, between science and glamour, between politics and style, or between the virtual and the physical; it is an exciting and dynamic field that is permanently under construction.

Lidewij Edelkoort, in collaboration with Lotte van Gelder, collected the beautiful pop-up works featured in this publication. Together with the essays and interviews, this book paints a captivating and exciting picture of a new generation in the throes of designing the future.

Temporary
It pops-up, it floats, it melts down. It is in process.
Static grids of modern and post-modern times have
given way to elastic, fluid and hybrid structures
and technological advancements have empowered
us to reach to the stars, and beyond. Design is
liberated from time constraints. In this fluid
contemporary period, it has become artistically
fashionable and socially acceptable to pick the
cherries of another man's labour and clone them,
blending them according to our own needs or
desires. Designers find themselves free to choose
any subject, material or approach. All are invited
into this open-source arena of creation.

Mobile
Tap into the stream and move along in any
direction of choice from wherever we are. Once
we step into these turbulent virtual waters,
various currents run at different speeds, and
a coloured spectrum of volatile information
splashes in your face. Step out of your own
comfort zone and dip into one of the many
infinite galaxies. It is up to you. Virtual
talismans will accompany you on your travels.
These clever devices, examples of progressive
technology, store your personal identity and give
you a home away from home.

Hybrid
We move from on-screen to off-screen with natural ease. The sharp edges between virtual and physical expressions are melting into an eclectic amalgam. In this fast-track process of evolution, the integration between man and technology has become a fact. Like techno-phibians we alternate between the different realities. In a time-span of merely two decades a world has risen where everything merges, mashes-up and mixes. In this concoction there is a niche for everything, and everyone.

D.I.Y.
Come join, and make your own! As we
shifted from vertical power-structures to
horizontal lines of communication, consumers
are becoming creators. Designers provide the
interface that enables you to shape your world
according to your own needs and taste. Creating
by sharing and exchanging. Develop your own
knowledge database or archive, or reinforce your
political voice with the help of on-line tools. No
need to do it all by yourself. Hop into the
flash-mob, plug-in to the virtual realm, criticize,
re-shape, recycle. It's give and take in this
on-line community.

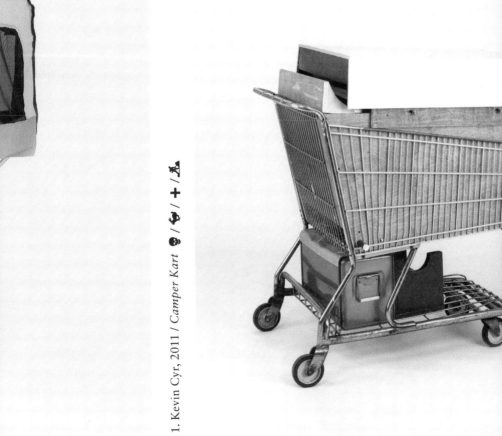

1. Kevin Cyr, 2011 / *Camper Kart* 🌐 / 🐦 / + / 💀

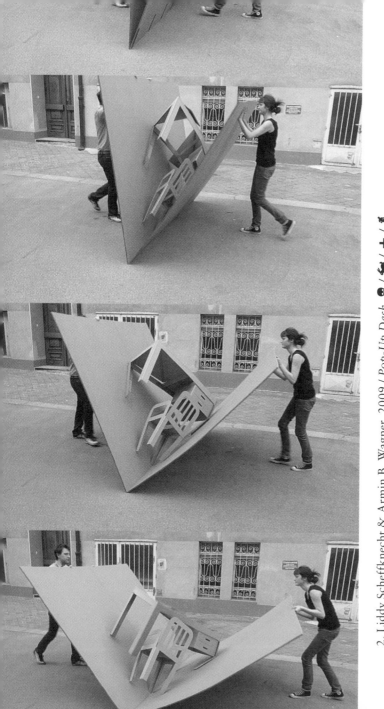

2. Liddy Scheffknecht & Armin B. Wagner, 2009 / *Pop-Up Desk* 🌑 / 🐾 / ✚ / ⚒

3. Saron Paz, 2007 / *Story Store* 🎭 / 🐾 / ⚞   *Photo credit: Rachel Griffen*

4. Sarah Oppenheimer, 2006 / 554-5251 🕮 / ✛ Courtesy of the artist and P.P.O.W. Gallery, New York. Photo credit: Kevin Noble

4. Sarah Oppenheimer, 2006 / MF-142 ⊕ / ✚   *Courtesy of the artist and Annely Juda Fine Art. Photo credit: Steven White*

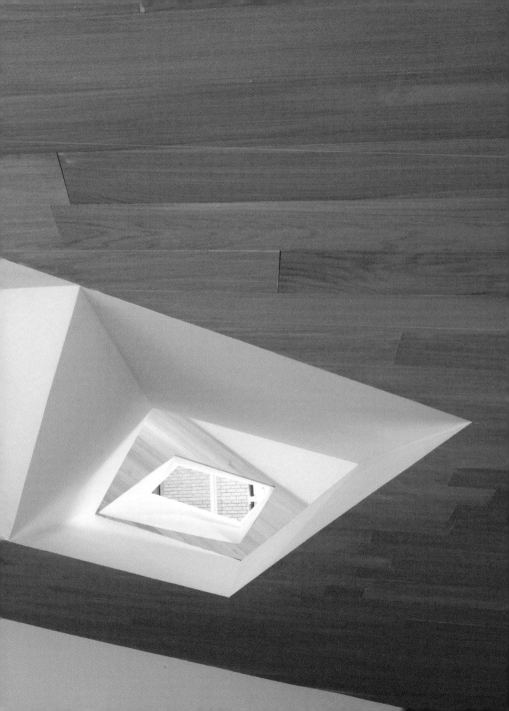

5. Eric Ku, 2010 / CHAIR/CHAIR 🌐 / 👤 / + / 🏃

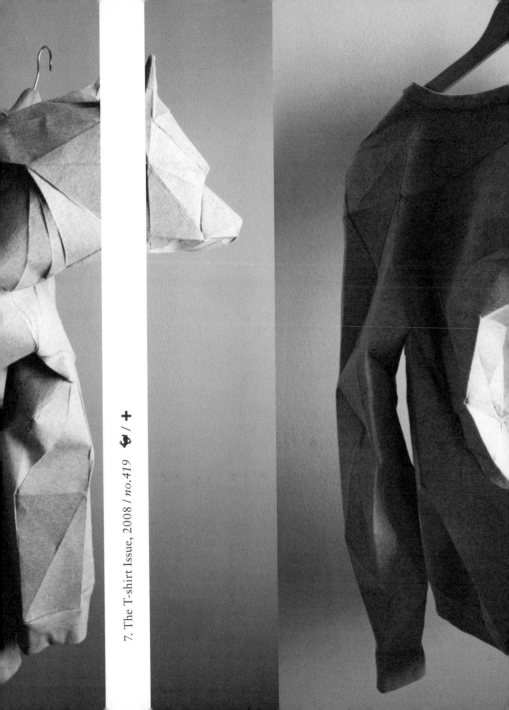

7. The T-shirt Issue, 2008 / *no.419* 🐸 / ✚

8. Rodrigo Solórzano, 2009 / *Big Gorilla-Dar Sabra* ✛

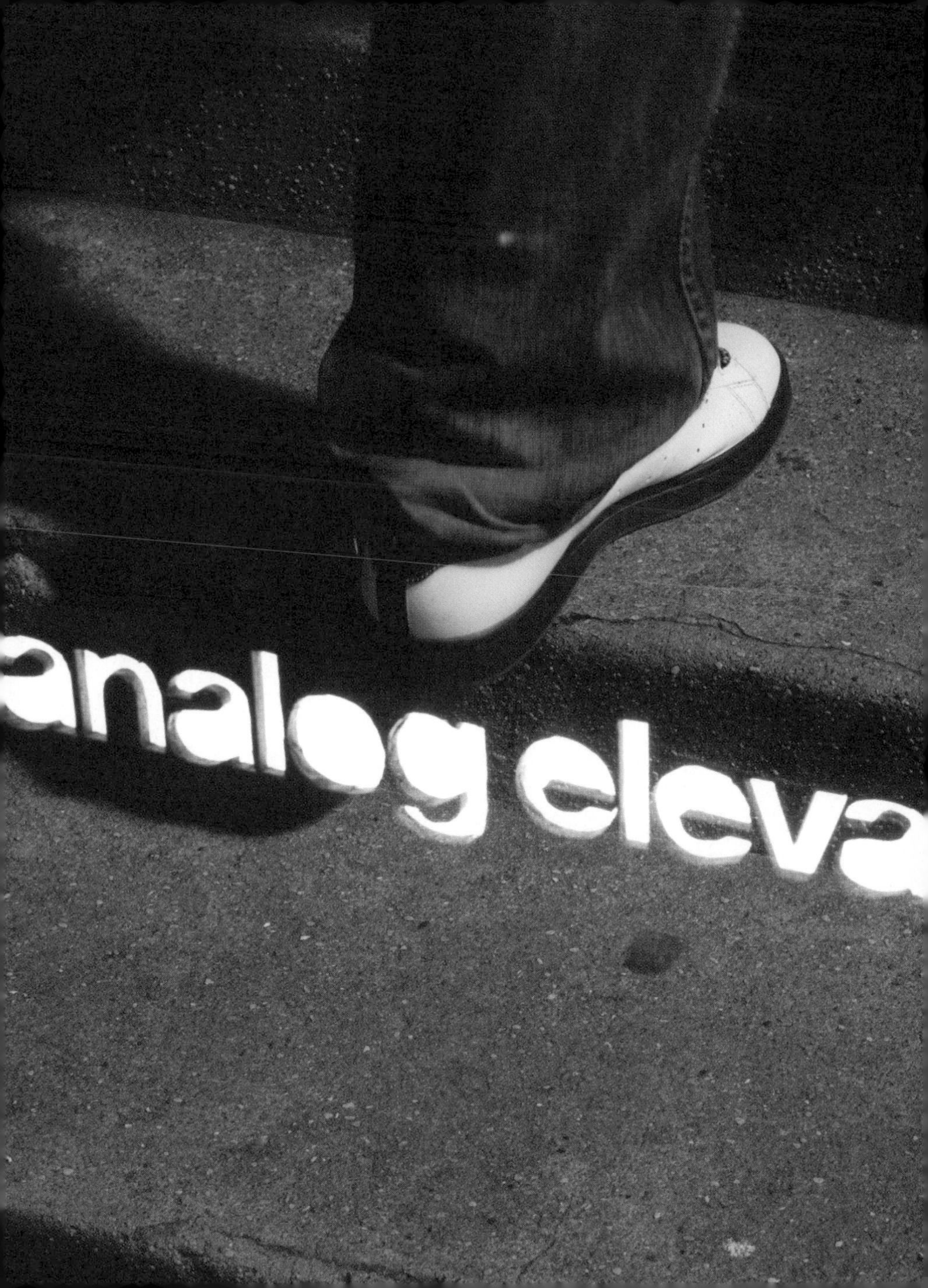
analog eleva

9. Analog Project, 2009 / *Analog Project* 🐌 / + / ♨

10. James Victore, 2003 / Hero-Victim Pins ☻ / + / ☠

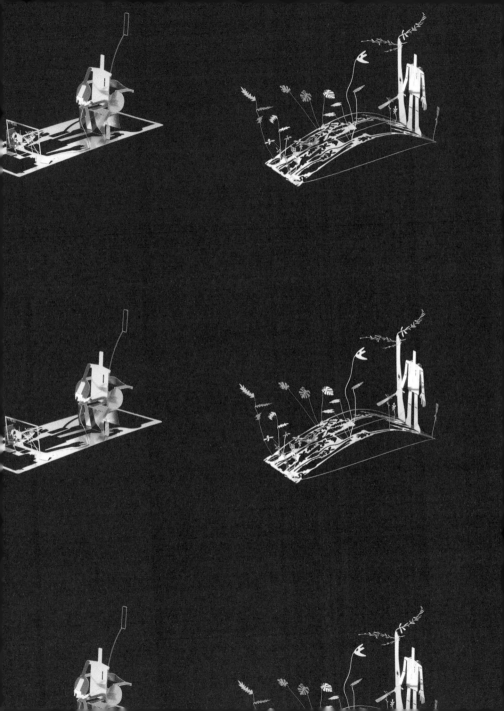

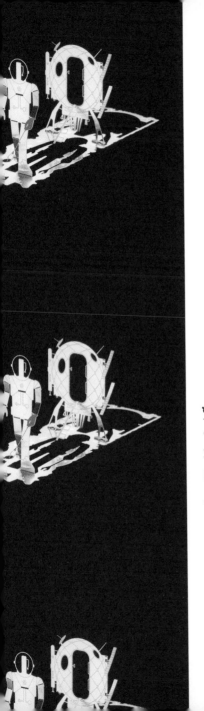
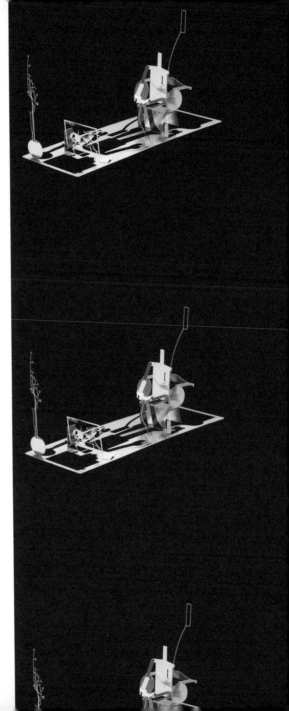

11. Sam Buxton, 2008 / *Mikro World* + / ⚒

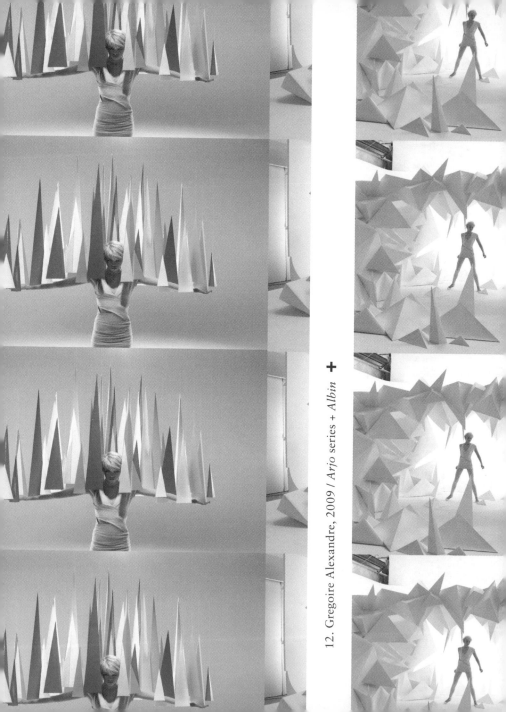

12. Gregoire Alexandre, 2009 / *Arjo series + Albin* +

13. Jaime Hayon, 2011 / sketches for ¿Que Pasa Guey? / in collaboration with Audax Textielmuseum Tilburg / Textiel.ab

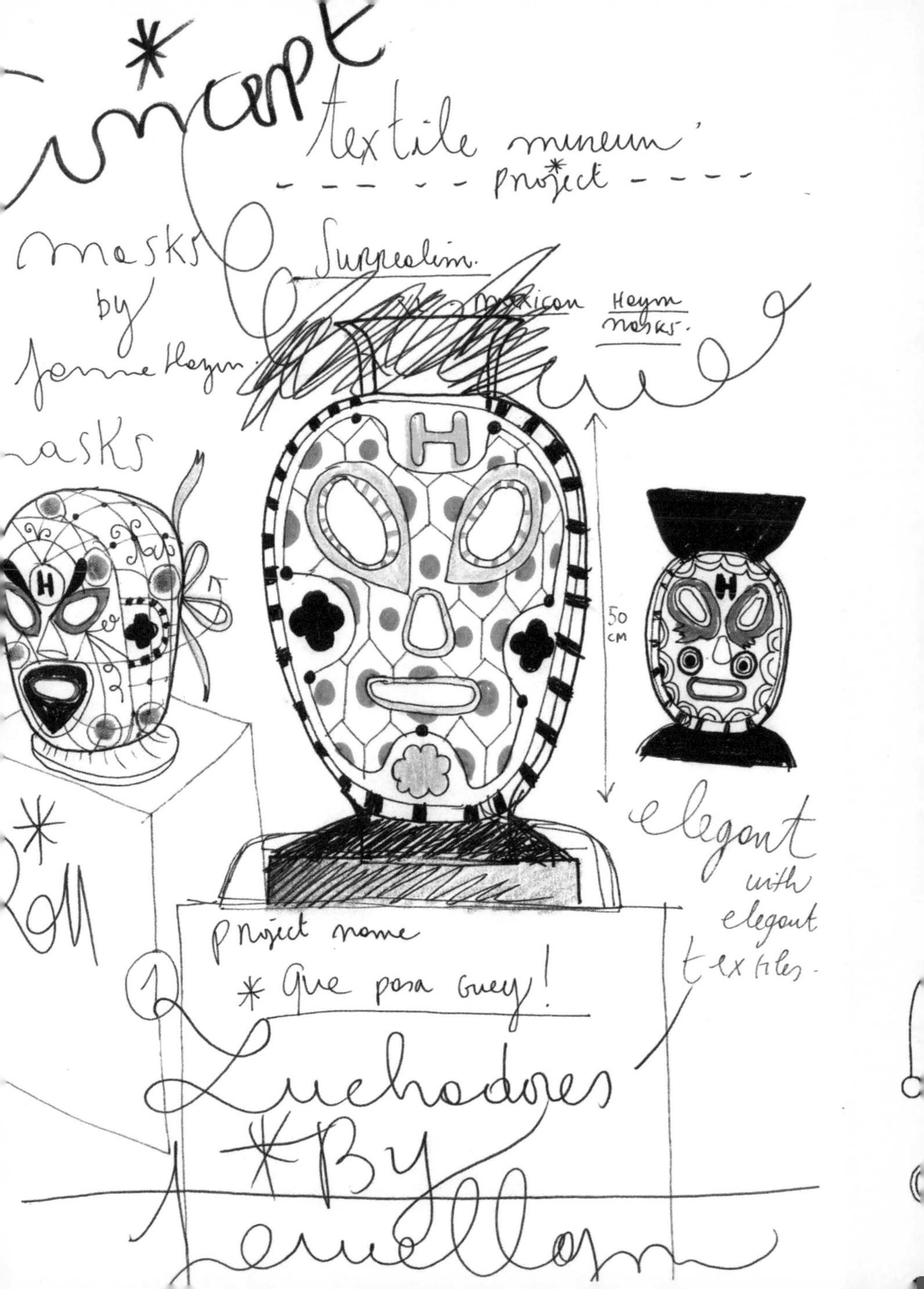

concept

Textile museum
- - - - project - - - -

masks
by
Jennie Heym

Surrealism.

Mexican Heym
masks.

H

50 cm

masks

elegant
with
elegant
textiles.

Project name
* Que pasa Guey!

Luchadores
* By
Jennie Heym

14. Eric Elms, 2011 / *Stay High* +

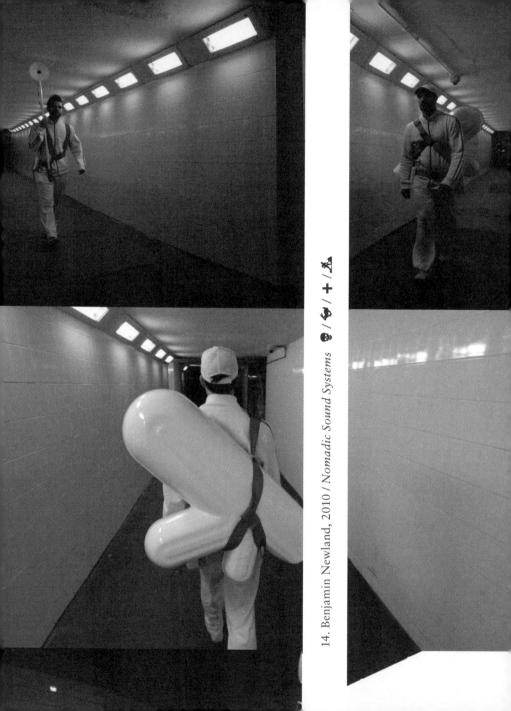

14. Benjamin Newland, 2010 / *Nomadic Sound Systems* ● / 🐾 / + / 🐎

15. Catharina van Eetvelde, 2011/ *ILK* ☻ / ⚓

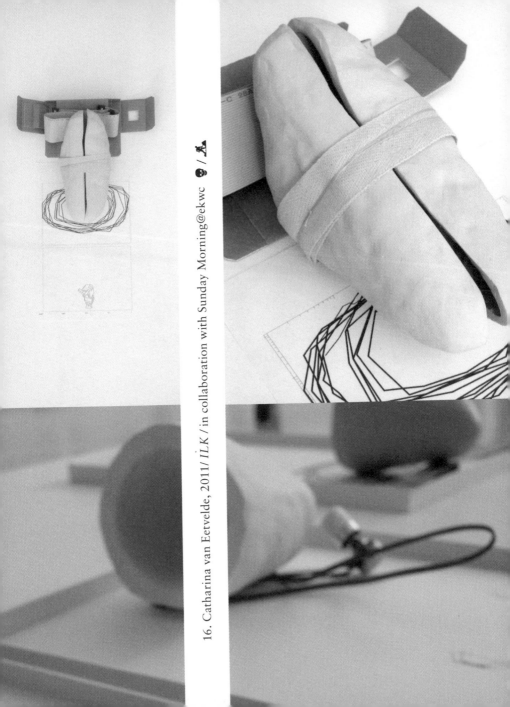

16. Catharina van Eetvelde, 2011/ *ILK* / in collaboration with Sunday Morning@ekwc 🐌 / ☠

17. Anna Garforth, 2010 / *Grow – Type Series* 💀 / ✛ / ⚑

UNLIMITED
URBAN
WOODS

Open: ma t/m zo 10:00 - 22:00

18. DUS Architects, 2011 / *Unlimited Urban Woods* 🌱 / 🐾 / 🐞 / ✚ *Photo credit: Pieter Kers*

19. Ex Studio, 2005 / *Dream House* 🌑 / 🐸 / +

20. Heatherwick Studios, 2004 / *Rolling Bridge* 🌐 / 🐾 / 🚶 / 🏛 / +

Photo credit: Steve Speller

21. Peter Callesen, 2009 / *Transparent God* **✝** / 🐎

21. Peter Callesen, 2010 / *White Window* + / 🏃

21. Peter Callesen, 2010 / *The End of the Road* + /

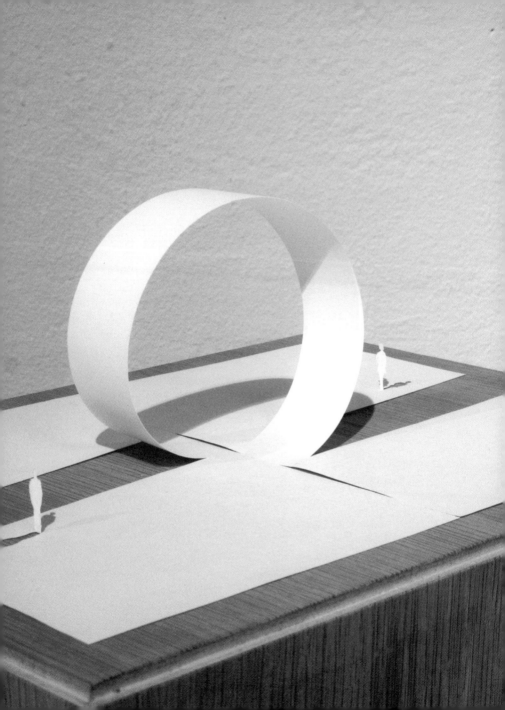

22. Chris Labrooy, 2011 / *Shrink Wrap Stills* +

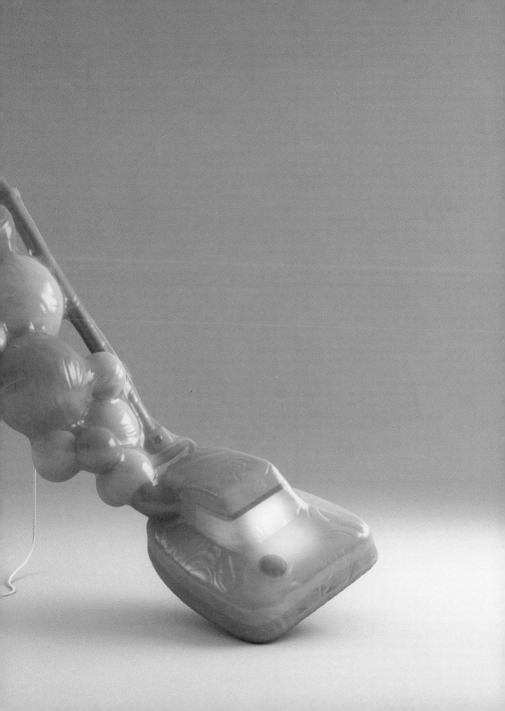

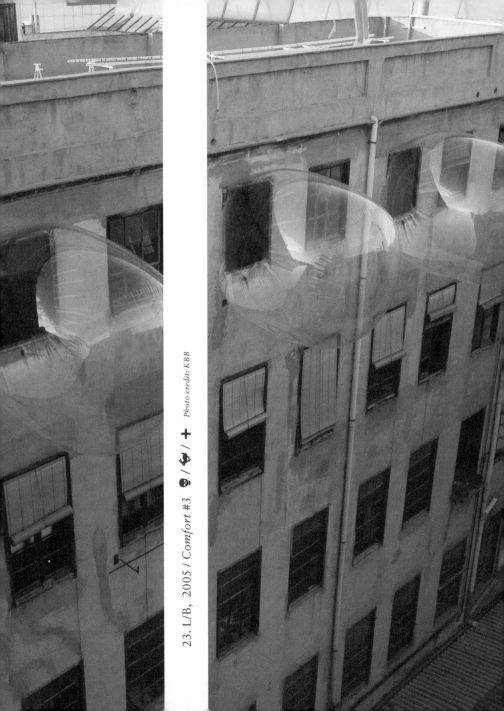

23. L/B, 2005 / Comfort #3 ☻ / 🐟 / ✚   *Photo credit: KBB*

24. Brad Downey, 2010 / The beginning and the End 😀 / ☠

25. Neozoon, 2009 / *Furry Sloth* 🐾 / 🦇 / + / 🏃

25. Neozoon, 2011 / *Knut* 😮 / 🐾 / + / 🐾

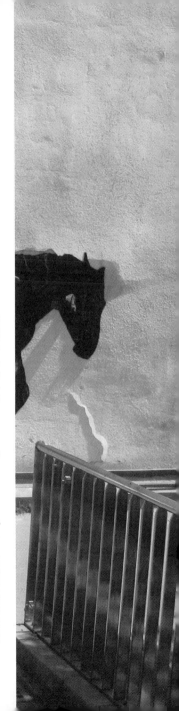

26. Niels Shoe Meulman, 2010 / *Throw Up Graffitti Cocktails* ✶ / ⚘

27. Laurens Manders, 2008 / *Hide* 🐦 / **+** / 🐜

Photo credit: Rene van der Hulst (exterior) & Tom Haga (interior)

28. Koosje Ruijgrok & Tessa Teixeira de Mattos, 2011 / *The Wild Folded* + *Photo credit: Karen Rosetzsky*

29. Yochai Matos, 2009 / *Flame Gate* 🔲

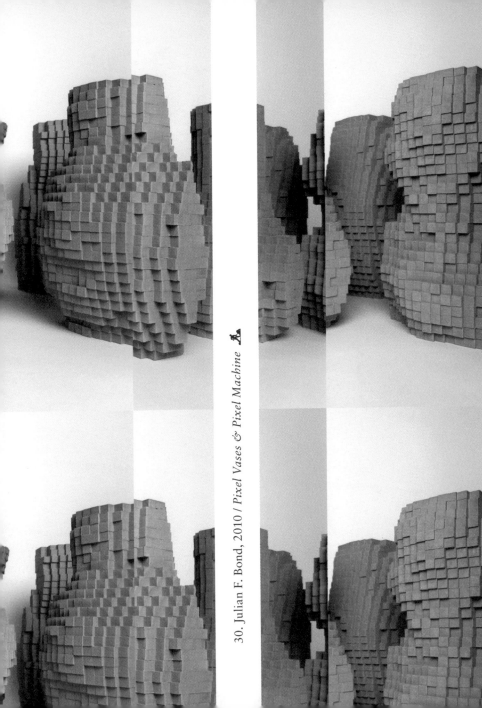

30. Julian F. Bond, 2010 / *Pixel Vases & Pixel Machine* 🐀

BEAM ME UP, SCOTTY
On toying with dimensions
By Lidewij Edelkoort

This still rather young century is going through
a huge shift in mentality that creates a growing
need to combine, to layer, to accumulate and then
to intimately blend that which has previously
been seen as contrasting. Becoming averse to
conflict and tired of straight linear programming
and obsolete bipolar thinking, a need is felt for
osmosis and a flexible form of unity, for bringing
together and fusing opposite ideas such as old and
new, young and old, individual and group, man
and woman, craft and industry, analogue and
virtual, as well as black and white. This fusing of
contrasts will together form a huge grey domain
in which neutral nuances will colour life diffused
and differently, a place where multiple variations
can develop, in which derivatives will be born and
hybrids can pop up to form new and unknown
species. Only then will the creativity of the 21st

1

century unleash itself and engulf us in inspiring events and actions and a flood of visual delight.

The youngest generations have a strong instinct for change and for adapting to disruption, accepting hybrids as natural and vital, embracing a radical new way of thinking that intimately adopts complexity and unpredictability. They are developing new instincts for survival in a society of organized instability. The one thing that will be required from these generations is a comfortable fluency with the disruptive energy that is shaping our world. A necessary rethinking of society is therefore in the making, in which the individual will donate his talent to the group without losing his own identity. This morphing of the self that occurs through coming together with others better prepares us for the roller-coaster times to come and constitutes an amazing evolution of society, the positive popping up of a promise of a better, modified world. These younger generations born into a life dominated by living, playing, learning and sleeping with screens

(TV, PC, Xbox, Pad and Pod) seem to exist in a shadow area, a no-man's land between the second and third dimension. This talented pop-up generation moves fluidly and easily between 2D and 3D as though they no longer notice that there is a difference. Their brains are trained to see volume in a flat sketch or to discern structure within volume; culture as the blueprint of an architect.

This is how a more imaginative world will develop, one that offers supple and flowing experiences, a world where the eye and the mind scan images in search of a reality to be found in a two-and-a-half dimension, accumulating layers of two-dimensional matter to produce the illusion of three; letting them pop up and fall flat in one simple movement of up and down, around and about, back and forth and moving in unison on the swing of existence.

Pop-up is possibly at once the most popular and the most despised system of creation: the pop-up children's book is fondly remembered and recently rekindled, while the pop-up window intrudes on our private research sphere and is therefore the most hated system in virtual existence. Both pop-up methods, though, have the capacity to surprise and to make us experience a moment of magic.

With the knowledge that our brain works like a rapid-prototyping software program which layers 2D to give the illusion of 3D, it remains to be seen how our impression of 3D will perform when encountering that other illusion of 3D broadcasting from our perfected high-tech and interactive screens. Will these double fictions eliminate each other, enter a duel of competing illusions or conversely will the layering reinforce the feeling of space and volume? Will the evidence pop up and unravel? Will the truth be felt that this is all but an illusion?

The process of contemporary creation gives proof of this movement, with a going back and forth between dimensions like a yo-yo on a creative string:

• The doodles and sketches flow fast and furious and seemingly without effort, with new ideas popping up constantly, helping the design discipline to take final form by anchoring the conceptual phase in a flat plane.

• The impeccable line-drawings that follow, directly executed on-screen, are extra flat and almost lifeless, giving them a cookie-cutter edge: flat yet suggesting a rebounding surface. Somehow evoking a cartoon.

• The final volume is obtained from the drawings through molding, pouring, sculpting, layering, folding or carving, and retains the cartoonish flatness of the drawings; yet it is round and chubby and takes up space. The eye and the brain want to discern both the 3D roundness and the flatness of the object, with the result that one seems to be penetrating into another more enchanted world. Therefore these techno talents appear to be constantly beaming up and down, between realities in a virtual and, at the same time, analogue play of dimensions.

The dynamism and ease of this pop-up mentality, its flexibility and versatility, are a source of inspiration for the idiom of graphic as well as industrial and autonomous design. All artistic disciplines begin to smash up, with the industrial designer doing animation and the communication designer making embroideries, the architect writing scenarios and the fashion designer creating sculptural form. Roles shift, connect and mingle to the extent that there seems to be only one universal and holistic artistic discipline that is popping up in strange places and moving constantly between dimensions, possibly searching for a newer one.

Suddenly I call to mind the most striking episodes of the iconic and futuristic Star Trek series, where a human body could be disintegrated into immaterial substance to reincarnate and pop up somewhere else, on another even more fascinating planet.... "Beam me up, Scotty", is still resonating, tickling our imagination with a future that is perfectly positioned between the existing dimensions and those other, still-to-be-discovered ones.

Nestled in this in-between area, a new flexible frame of refracting time with adventurous unknown work is being prepared; elastic artistic statements that are moving between all disciplines and all dimensions, loosening up all rules and regulations. Knitting buildings from within, molding second-skin textiles and pleating matter into mind. Traveling back in time to study archaeology and repeat the organic structures of building and the square structures of dress in ancient civilizations. Our devotion to detail will bring the square alive and will fold the garment into sculptural form, able to wrap geometry into complexity. Resulting in clothes that are made like architecture folded along computerized origami, with computer-animated machines narrating fairytales, with dimensional typography taking craft's centre stage and with high-tech systems emulating the romantic random movements of a new nature. The age of pop-up is becoming reality.

The invention of the Wii interactive computer games by Miyamoto has forever changed the landscape of gaming, popping the couch potatoes up to life and into action and into a slimmer frame, generating 3D action from a 2D device. The physical intimacy of the 2.5D is yet to be discerned and measured.

This is why and how the members of this pop-up generation need new stimuli that will often be manifested via a definitively temporary, often immaterial or sustainable re-usable nature. Pop-up parties, pop-up shops and pop-up museums are a first fluid attempt to randomly satisfy this need for the nomadic trail hovering between the dimensions of existence, as if aiming to live detached from everyday reality while entering a new one.

Another and next step are guerrilla brands and gorilla marathons that only appear for a short period of time and then disappear into nothingness or fade into otherness, like the guerrilla knitting organizations around the globe that are covering — with fetishist fervor and in wonderful fluffy yarns — street objects and urban furniture as well as innocent passers-by. This attempt to cuddle society from within brings tenderness and togetherness to public space, attaching all people with one strand of yarn, creating together the fabric of life.

Other public expressions of popping up may be related to food sharing and urban farming or the reconstruction of the past to become the future, with collectives reincarnating the use of such discarded materials as vintage fur coats to give them another life as animated and animistic bas-reliefs of roaring wildness. Making graffiti come alive and kicking, popping up with an instinct for volume and political narration.

Epilogue
Seen from today's perspectives it is possible and even plausible that we will later turn towards a flattening of volume, to lay all matter open and horizontal as if to have a better overview of the possibilities, in order

to landscape the innovation and creative dimensions for the future as if it were a Japanese stamp. Flat planes patiently waiting to eventually pop up and unfold to spread their wings. Like a paper plane* penetrating the brain, hitting the grey matter with twin-tower magnitude, announcing another period of eagle-ish spread-out overall thinking, able to observe in 360 degrees, seemingly unhindered by the need for the presence of volume. Voting for vision instead.

Working with sense-surround radar, able to discern ideas on a more mental dimension, playing with telepathy and fantasy; writing about dimensions, picturing dimensions, sound-scaping dimensions and imagining dimensions without realizing them. Savouring taste without ownership.

Remembering Flatland, by E. A. Abbot, the fascinating famous novel on flatness written in 1884, that tries to teach the reader how to eat, play and dress flat and thus brings us, suddenly one night, into virtual contact with an equally flat alien from outer space.

Please beam me up, Scotty,
I am more than ready!

Lidewij Edelkoort

* *In January 2008 a paper origami space-plane
was unveiled, to be launched into orbit later in
the century. It is able to withstand extreme heat
because of its lightness. No launch date has been
set, but Professor Shinji Suzuki, an aerospace
engineering professor at Tokyo University, is
positive and optimistic, hoping that the space
station crew will write a message of peace on the
eight-centimeter plane, to be read by whoever
finds the plane upon its return to earth.*

OF ARTS, BRAINS AND REALITIES
By Ahmed El Hady

Have you ever thought about what is happening
in our brains when we look at the world around
us? How do we distinguish between different
objects in the universe we live in? How can
we explore our reality and interact with it in
a continuous manner? We are embedded in a
continuum of scenes as if it is a movie running
at a speed faster that we can perceive. Indeed,
our lives as perceptual experiences are just
static images put together one after the other
that run at a very high speed that makes us feel
that it is continuous. One might think of our
reality as two-dimensional sheets that when
put sequentially are giving us the sense or the
delusion of a three-dimensional universe as if we
are living in a continuous trompe l'oeil universe.
What we perceive as three-dimensional is only
an accumulation of two-dimensional projections.
How is this happening? De facto we are only

conscious of the results of a complex process that is happening in our brain.

When the light reflected on an object reaches our retina, a two-dimensional map or sheet of the basic object's features like edges and length is formed on our retina; the two-dimensional map travels through our neuronal highways to intermediate areas in our brain where texture and depth is added to the object's features forming a two and a half dimensional map. This 2.5D map finds its way to the higher brain areas where more complex object features are extracted and recognized by many specialized areas: colour is acknowledged in one space, motion in another, the same for orientation and further complex characteristic features of the object. It is striking to realize that, for example, colour is just a concept emerging from our brains making use of the different light wavelengths. This casts doubt on an objective non-distorted perception of reality. Reality in this way is constructed from brain concepts. The different object's features that have been processed in different brain areas will then be interpolated and projected to appear like a 3D object. It is amazing how our brain processes each feature of an object in parallel systems separated in space and time. Then, these parallel distributed processes are bound into a single object that we perceive. But is this enough for object recognition? No, it isn't; you can form a 3D imagery of an object but you do not recognize it. For this we need our memory system that has learned via experience a set of stored objects with their semantic meanings. Since childhood, our brain has been exploring, learning and experiencing objects and has been imposing a semantic meaning on it. Our brain makes use of these stored views by comparing the perceived three-dimensional object to the already stored information in order to recognize it. Our brains therefore depend on our early experience of reality and are in a continuous learning experience in order to deal with novelty. Just to clarify more what the brain is doing, one can look at the brain as a group of systems that abstract basic characteristics and strive to form a concept of the object perceived. However the brain has to learn the process of abstraction by perceiving many particulars. What if the brain has an incomplete grasp on reality in its abstraction process? What if the utopia of our lives is not attained? What if our immediate experience of reality is not satisfactory?

In order to address these questions, one finds refuge in creation. The greatest thing about arts and design is that creative people can transform their own frustration, dissatisfaction or imagination into a work of art whether it is a musical, a ballet, a novel, a sculpture or a design. Through design one can transgress the abstraction process that the brain uses and produce novel forms and innovative concepts.

One might say: isn't the creative work just an object like others? The answer is that the perception of the artwork is not the same as the perception of mundane everyday objects.

A creative work is a live object that has a subjective dimension. It is an object that embodies the experience of a designer or artist, his or her own attempt to transgress reality and create novel abstractions and alternative realities. The ingenuity of a creative form is in eliciting multiple interpretations as if our brains stand confused on how to abstract it. Our perception of design is as distinct as it is accompanied by the very subjective experience of beauty and empathy that our brain generates. It is by this way that artists and designers themselves become teachers that train the brains of their audiences in novel ways. They help them to learn newer forms of abstractions. On the long term, art works might help people to build novel realities and perceptual experiences. After all, just to remind us again, reality is a construction of our own brains. Through creative work, the limit of the possible is extended and stretched in ways no one can imagine. Take today's kids, raised in front of multiple flat screens and touch screens where they are immersed in virtual realities; one can imagine that their perception will undergo a dimensionality reduction in time. One can begin to raise a fundamental question about our own reality: do we really live in a 3D world or do we live in a trompe l'oeil world? Is our continuous interaction with smart phones, computers and other flat objects going to change the dimensions of our world? Is this process reversible?

It is amazing to realize that with all of this happening without our interference, we are just observers of our own reality while our brain with its great plasticity is being continuously changed. All of these processes by which our brain perceives objects are shaped by and shape the designs and cultural artefacts our civilization is producing. In our designs we download our unconscious unreachable reality and through design, novel realities are uploaded into our brains. This dialogue between our brain and our cultural expressions is crucial and unavoidable; as our brains are the windows to the world we live in, these windows are either extended or reduced or manipulated by changes in the world around us.

In my opinion, artists, designers, neuroscientists and philosophers are all doing the same job; they are studying and changing our brains, making use of its plasticity and its ability to abstract reality, only their tools are different. Artists and designers use their creative revolutionary talents and innovative designs, neuroscientists use their experimental and scientific empirical tools, while philosophers use novel generative ideas. I just want you for a moment to imagine these multi-stage intricate complex mechanisms that are allowing you to see and to read the very text you are reading now; so you will realize how much we are unaware of the complexity underlying our own perception of existence. Nevertheless, despite this complexity, we can potentially use or strengthen these complex mechanisms by improved interaction with reality. Such an augmented interaction with reality can be realized with designs that enhance brain activity, teaching it novel patterns and extending its memory of stored views. It is very instructive here for artists, designers and neuroscientists to work side by side to explore the never-ending potential of our brains. We still have a long way to go, but with our current state of knowledge, we know that our brains shape our reality in the same way that reality shapes our brains. At the end, I will leave you to imagine what our future post-human, design and brain will look like? Will they be separable?

Ahmed El Hady is a graduate student at the Max Planck institute for dynamics and self organization, where he is working on a neurotechnology project trying to understand and control neuronal network dynamics.

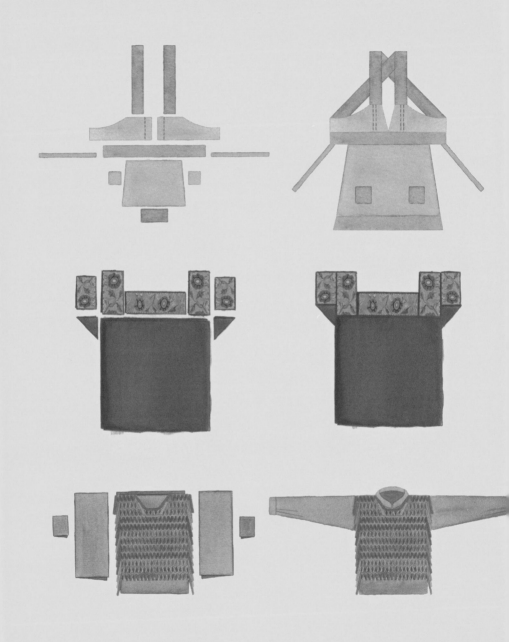

THE EVOLUTION OF THE SQUARE
By Carla Fernández

POP-UP 1. Square Roots
While in university I worked at the Museum of
Mexican Indigenous Fashion, a job that granted
me access to the collection of cultural heritage.
I delved into their archives to precisely study
the way that all the different costumes had
been constructed. As one couldn't actually take
the clothes apart, I traced all their seams and
pleats with a pencil and paper. These exercises
of deconstruction lead me to get to know these
pieces by heart. To my great surprise almost all
of these complicated garments could be reduced
to rectangles or squares, making each and every
piece of cloth parallel. The geometric shapes
would be folded and pleated to pop up into
clothes that would take form around the body.
It were precisely these shapes in the
clothes that connected my fashion studies to my
art history degree; as I got to know the basics of

my profession from a theoretical as well as from
a practical side. From the start I had been
interested in the early vanguard-movement, more
specifically the artists that focused on clothing
design like the uniforms designed by Tatlin,
Stepanova and Lemanova amongst other
Constructivists, the anti-neutral clothing manifest
of the Futurists Balla and Marinetti, Malevich's
geometric theatre costumes and the graphic
fashion creations by Sonia Delauney.

Through my newly attained focus and
research I started to consider indigenous
heritage not solely as something primitive,
but more for its constructive and architectural
quality. I could also demonstrate that contrary
to the kitsch stereotype that is exported about
Mexico; ancient patterning is an incredible
elaborate system of pleats, folds and seams
that construct a vast array of garments using
squares and rectangles only. This has been the
source of inspiration to our label.

POP-UP 2. Design
Many other cultures' fashions, like the Hindu,
Japanese and Peruvian, or even traditional
European clothing like the Dutch aprons and
skirts, use the square as a base for their patterns.
I always asked myself why this is a constant, and
the first question has to do with the beginning
of fashion; the fabric. If one takes Mexico as an
example and the complicated and long process of
making hand-made fabrics with waist loom, one
understands the meaning of fabric as an open
book that tells the story of the weaver that made
it. If we cut a page and divide it with seams we
would not read the entire story.

I also believe when you have a square
garment, you can play more with it; in Mexico
one finds garments that can become a skirt
during the day, or a bed cover by night. I believe
that the freedom that the geometrical clothing
gives the wearer and the fact that they can
become part of the creative process depending
on how they want to use it, is what makes these

garments so contemporary. They adapt to their wearer and his or her imagination or individual fashion expression.

For us tradition is not static and fashion is not ephemeral.

Even though many countries have the same geometrical basis for their traditional clothing, Mexican pattern making is still quite unique; from the Spanish Conquista onwards, the garments would follow the western tradition of shaping the clothing along the lines of the body. However the pre-Hispanic tradition of the same time also kept evolving into an even more intricate play of shapes: starting from the square and the rectangle, fabric was manipulated through pleats, pegs and folds to imitate the new outfits that the Conquistadores had brought with them; indigenous culture cloning western dress. The result was a type of textile origami. Until today, the use of weaving from a small loom is continued, and with this, the techniques of ornamenting according to this specific geometry.

While working in these archives, I found myself faced with the DNA of Mexico's cultural heritage and realized that I could simply tap into this material as a source of inspiration. Another option I encountered, however, was working directly with the indigenous craft communities and to create contemporary designs with them. This is how Taller Flora came to being.

POP-UP 3. Mobile Laboratory
Taller Flora is a mobile fashion laboratory that travels through Mexico visiting indigenous communities, especially women co-ops creators of handmade textiles.

When I started working with groups of indigenous artisans, I realized it would be impossible to teach them western dressmaking techniques. The first obstacle was language: in a co-op of eight women, it was possible that none or only one of them spoke Spanish, and hence an interpreter was needed. Centimetres and inches were another cultural convention that was sometimes awkward: instead, they used fingers, palms and forearms as measurements.

At that point I understood that it was natural to use the codes that indigenous people already master; I had to spend an intensive period of time observing their systems to become familiar with them. If I wanted to teach, I first had to learn. This is how a parallel process arose, an organic pedagogy whose basis is above all visual–a hybrid between mimicry and pop-up clothing based on the square pattern. We would show in one community how 40 other ethnic groups around Mexico use the pattern-making system of squares and rectangles. As they make their own garments with this same basis, they would observe the possibilities of system and therefore make new designs using their own methods in only three or four sessions.

The method has the following advantages:

- Artisans are artists. They can introduce changes and invent new styles based on what they do best.

- If artisans are using a method that is familiar to them, they can create their own prototypes for new garments.

- Creative people make original designs. Those who introduce new designs are likely to also improve their businesses.

- It avoids turning co-ops into sweatshops that manufacture other people's designs.

POP-UP 4. Pop-Up Store
This folding structure is an exhibition display
made for us by Mexican artist Pedro Reyes. It
blends the function of a pop-up store with the
features of a pop-up book; elements such as
tunnels, flaps, pull-tabs, pop-outs, pull-downs,
etc. It performs all the requirements of a portable
store: showroom, dressing room, cashier, storage,
racks, shelves, mirrored rooms etc. When folded,
the structure can be shipped to a different site
minimizing the materials used in every new venue.

Being part of a museum exhibition, the
pop-up store activates a real economy in the
exhibition space. For me, fashion is only fully
experienced if the public can try and test a
garment of their choice, knowing they can
acquire any of the pieces in stock.

The social mission of the label has a long-
term commitment to the indigenous communities
that participate in the making of the clothes. In
this sense, an exhibition space is a good
opportunity to explain the elaborate

craftsmanship process required for the completion of each garment.

Carla Fernández is a fashion designer and entrepreneur based in Mexico City. From her mobile workshop Taller Flora she creates new designs based on indigenous techniques and practices, collaborating with different artisans from the various ethnic groups in her country.

THE CHANGING URBAN LANDSCAPE:
My Three Cities
By Bruce Sterling

Here in the second decade of the century, I pursue a newfangled 'multilocative' lifestyle. Beograd is the home of Boris Srebro, a gloomy and acerbic writer of Eastern European fantastyka. Torino hosts Bruno Argento, an artsy Italian fantascienza writer with a yen for European high-tech. And Austin, capital of Texas, is the home of American cyberpunk writer Bruce Sterling.

The Balkans, southern Europe and Texas have exceedingly disparate backgrounds. It follows that strong resemblances between the three cities are aspects of modernity.

I like to call the temperament of the twenty-teens 'Dark Euphoria', and I think that it clusters around two cultural poles I call 'Gothic High-Tech' and 'Favela Chic'. These are a novelist's verbal shorthand for forms of behaviour forced on us by vagaries of modern infrastructure. 'Gothic High-Tech' is Gothic in the Edgar Allan Poe sense: abandoned, hollowed-out, haunted, broke, decadent. 'Favela Chic' is chic in the sense of popular, modish, rapid, new and unproven.

All modern cities have some aspects of Gothic High-Tech. These are commonly analogue industries that have been obsolesced or offshored, leading to their collapse or re-use by alien enterprises. They also all feature Favela Chic zones where semi-legal, immaterialized, highly inventive conniving is the order of the day.

A descriptive of this kind can seem abstract, so, for the remainder of this essay, let me illustrate it through example. Torino, Beograd, and Austin, for all their differences, are physically quite similar. They are inland regional capitals of similar population sizes, situated on similar rivers: the Danube, the Po and the Colorado.

Like a shark, a porpoise and a mosasaur, they have roughly the same responsive capacity to the pressures of contemporary events. Let's consider some of these responses.

INNOVATIVE HOUSING.
Beograd: splavovi.
Torino: stuffed animal.
Austin: tech incubator.

The Beograd 'splav' is a houseboat perched on the banks of the Danube. Due to flaws in Belgrade's primitive post-communist real-estate relations, it's easy to get away with a wide variety of gray-market entertainments on these makeshift boats and barges. So these wallowing restaurants, nightclubs and speakeasies have become a major source of the town's reviving tourist economy. Stylish, popular, cheap and poorly regulated, but also advanced, modish and popular with youth, splavovi are Favela Chic.

Torino is a former automobile manufacturing hub cratered by Asian competition. This created a huge industrial acreage that will be beset with Gothic bats and rats if not reoccupied. The result is the 'stuffed animal', a building created for some ostensibly serious purpose whose modern inhabitants are doing something else entirely. The 'Eataly' Slow Food market, occupying the hollowed bowels of a former FIAT plant, is classic Gothic High-Tech.

The Austin 'tech incubator' is a garage or fly-by-night numbered cubbyhole occupied by gamer or web-developer start-ups. They are very plug-and-play. Most tech start-ups die rapidly but are quickly replaced by others with a similar ethos and the same personnel.

Splavovi, stuffed animals and incubators, despite their shabbiness, all make money - commonly more for those who tolerate them than for those working inside them.

URBAN-RURAL RELATIONS.
Beograd: rural depopulation.
Torino: EU regulation.
Austin: environmental disaster.

Since Belgrade is more prosperous than the ethnically menaced Serbian hinterlands, it acts as a population sump. The agricultural areas that once supported the city are in collapse as rural villages fill with the elderly. One response is to attempt to reclassify Serbia's derelict areas as magnets for green tourism.

Torino's immediate surroundings benefit from generous, time-honoured EU agricultural subsidies, leading to a Disney-fied rural hinterland of wine lakes and butter seas. Less productive villages are in rapid demographic decay.

Austin is suffering an environmental disaster in which sustained drought, unheard-of summer temperatures and raging wildfires are destroying crops and cattle. Since water policies favour Texan cities, this intensifies urbanization, at least until the wells and reservoirs give out.

SHADOWY OVERCLASS
Beograd: natural-gas moguls, secret police.
Torino: car moguls, parliamentary fixers.
Austin: oil moguls, war-on-terror Tea Party.

POVERTY HOUSING.
Beograd: gypsy dumps.
Torino: immigrant neighbourhoods.
Austin: barrios and ghettos.

Nine percent of the Beograd population is Romany.
Since they double as trash-pickers, they tend to
live in makeshift housing in dumps. These are
classic favelas of an underclass without access to
property relations, except with the odd note that
these junk-homes are often made of high-tech
debris such as waterproof signage vinyl.

Torino lost a third of its population to
blue-collar decline in its auto manufacturing,
but instead of shrinking toward death like
Detroit, Torino liberalized immigration. This
policy attracted clusters of Libyans, Somali,

Ethiopians and other non-Italo-speaking populations, such as Bangladeshis, Peruvians and offshore Chinese. These migrants tend to flock together, not in pure ethnic enclaves, but in weirdly globalized foreigner enclaves where everybody does everybody else's laundry while speaking pidgin Italian.

Austin, as a historic consequence of slavery and Mexican secession, has had Mexican and black segregation areas since its year zero. The ethnic borders ooze around with the decades, but everybody knows who belongs where, except for Austin's immigrants, who are everywhere unsure of all such unspoken rules.

CHIC CONSUMER STREETS.
Beograd: Knez Mihajlova.
Torino: Via Roma.
Austin: Congress Avenue.

Belgrade's Knez Mihajlova street is a power axis that leads from the city's ancient river fortress toward its upgraded capital building. It's been ground zero for the Serbian transition to consumer capitalism, and is the prestige address for global retailers. Occasional riots, demos and other financial setbacks haven't been able to halt its relentless gentrification, although the modern street is markedly less genteel than it was during the Austro-Hungarian empire.

Torino's Via Roma is a Savoyard royalist marble arcade, infested with the cream of La Moda. It sells high heels and incendiary lingerie to Swiss and German housewives.

Congress Avenue is an Austin power coalition uniting politics, education and banking. Since most Austinites prefer to dress in rags, Congress Avenue never caught on as a prestige shopping district, but it's got plenty of bars and cosmic-cowboy honky-tonks.

FESTIVALS FOR FOREIGNERS
Beograd: beer festivals, huge music festivals, and (recently) a high-tech festival.
Torino: huge food festivals and high-tech festivals.
Austin: huge music festivals and huge high-tech festivals.

SOUVENIR CLOTHING
Beograd: aggressive Serbian nationalist-peasant gear, heroic sports-fan aspirational finery.
Torino: top-end shoes and lingerie.
Austin: country-western warehouse outlets.

VISITOR DEMOGRAPHICS
Beograd: Eastern Europeans, fellow ex-Yugoslavs, Danube boaters.
Torino: Swiss, Germans, French, Austrians, some wealthy Arabs and Russians.
Austin: US snowbirds, Mexicans, German cowboy tourists.

ZOMBIE AREAS
Beograd: un-rentable ex-Communist workers' housing barracks; NATO bombed zones.
Torino: abandoned, unfixable UNESCO world-heritage brick baroque heaps; derelict heavy industry barracks.
Austin: former railway-packing districts, derelict fossil-fuel plants, abandoned airport, flood-prone creek zones.

STYLISH ANTIQUE AREAS
Beograd: Zemun, Kralja Petra
Torino: Stile Floreale district
Austin: Hyde Park, Travis Heights
All these disparate areas flourished during the Belle
Epoque, and have never had to struggle much to
outmatch successor districts built in more difficult eras.

OFFICIAL FUTURE
Beograd: law-abiding, prosperous capital of
functional European state.
Torino: former Italian royal capital assumes
permanent shadow role as Italy's 'industrial
capital', 'media capital', 'cultural capital', 'creative
capital' or anything else that is seasonally modish
among Piedmontese urban planners.
Austin: curse-of-oil capital as clean-energy capital;
Austin Kept Weird as the Hicksville of the
Creative Class.

This essay should be ended with a thought
experiment. These cities indeed seem very

different, and, in their daily routines, very little unite them. If any one of them were suddenly annihilated, the effect on the other two would be minimal.

However, now imagine that these three modern urban populations were magically divided into thirds and scattered among all three cities. In other words, imagine that Beograd becomes a polyglot city that is Serbian-Texan-Italian, while Torino is fantastically Italian-Serbian-Texan, and Austin is magically Texan-Italian-Serbian.

Obviously, there would be some confusion about this rearrangement — for about six weeks.

After that transition, however, Belgrade would be blessed with a relatively sober, politically capable, technically advanced population. Sombre Torino would be completely electrified and dynamized. Austin would become the most sophisticated and soulful city in the American South.

Most every modern law and regulation rules against a global coup of this kind ever occurring. But imagine it happening. It would harm nothing, and deny these cities nothing that they want. It wouldn't even slow them down.

Nor, I wager, would these three cities become more alike — more globalized, more 'flattened'. With their ambitions fertilized and their logjams removed, they'd be LESS alike than they were before.

Bruce Sterling presents accurate descriptions of raw future scenarios with such elegance and wit that even dystopia becomes appealing. Sterling teaches at the European Graduate School and founded the Viridian Design Movement, an environmental aesthetic movement founded on the ideas of global citizenship, environmental design and techno-progressiveness.

How Ideas Pop Up
By Dr. Martine Naillon

Before we begin to explain how ideas and thoughts take shape in the brain, first let's take a small look at some of the brain's basic functions. The brain is a complex 'machine' with hundreds of functionalities. We will investigate and clarify only one, neurotransmission, to explain thought.

The brain consists of two components: the lobes, 'engines' that process information, and the neurotransmitters which is the information we absorb from the outside world and store in our brain for immediate or future use. The lobes are the 'thinking matter' and the neurotransmitters generate the electrical signals that activate the thinking process. The lobes are composed of neurons linked together via small bridges (synapses). On each side of these bridges, neurotransmitters accumulate, creating electric signals that propagate in the brain, (see image).

When information from the outside world is captured by one of your five senses, such as vision, it creates an accumulation of neurotransmitters. The information is then processed by different lobes. Each lobe has a specific cognitive function; the occipital lobe, for instance, processes visual signals while the parieto-temporal lobe processes the context of the information. For example: when you see a tiger, the emotion center in your brain (thalamus) triggers an instinctive memory of danger. Your body is ready to run, your heart accelerates and your muscles tighten. This creates an electric signal in your brain that carries this information to the vision center (occipital lobe) and then to the context analyzing center (parieto-temporal lobe). At this point, the context center detects that the tiger is behind bars and influences the decision center (frontal lobe) not to run. The thinking process can be illustrated as a succession of links between pieces of information that together create a 'decisional track'.

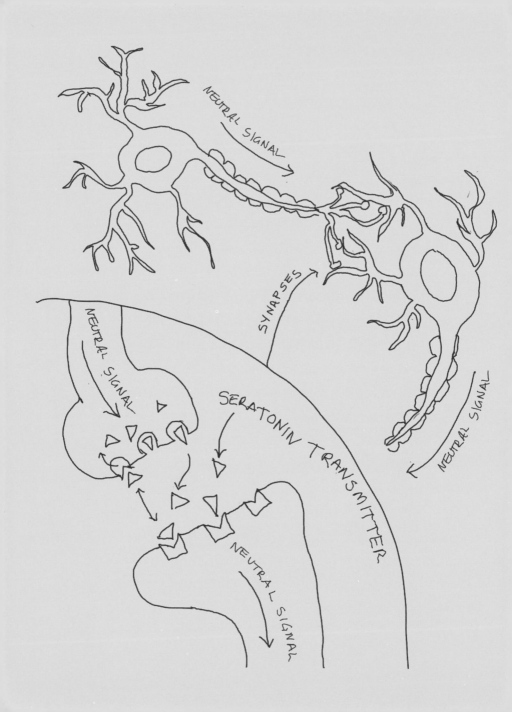

Analogy with condensed matter
The physical world consists of particles. When
these particles aggregate, they form a solid
condensed matter. Before becoming condensed,
matter can be in liquid or gas state. The difference
between the three states lies in the distance
between particles and the looseness with which
they are linked.

There is a critical temperature at which
matter changes its state. The instant matter
changes from liquid to solid, is called
'crystallization'. This is the instant in which the
distance between particles is secured and 'shapes'
and features of objects are created. Our brain is
trained to recognize and name these features.
When a designer creates a shape with his hands,
he has previously generated the shape in his brain.
Because he is an artist, he knows how to extract
it from his brain and transform it into a visible
and touchable shape. It is exactly in the same way
that thoughts are developed and ideas 'pop up'.

Thought: Aggregation of particles of knowledge
So, the world consists of particles in a solid, liquid
or gas state that our brain is trained to extract
and give meaning to, and develop them into
'particles of knowledge'. These particles are 'dots
of thought' that penetrate our brain and transform
into neurotransmitters. The thinking process
starts as a flow of electrical signals. Then the
neurotransmitters aggregate, 'connect the dots' of
knowledge, constitute shapes and reasoning, and,
suddenly, 'crystallize'. Ergo: the thought develops
from a flow of electrical signals to become a
condensed shape. An idea has popped up!

When an idea pops up, it is the
accumulation of days, months and years of
gathering information that enters the brain,
developing itself into neurotransmitter
accumulations. This process is subconscious and
only becomes conscious when the crystallization
pops up. It is called the 'light bulb effect'.

Pop-Up Generation: a new kind of
zapping intelligence

The brain of some people, such as scientists, anthropologists, creators or inventors, the so-called 'deep-thinkers', have the ability to extract prospective information from the outside world. These people have the courage to wander into unknown and informal spaces and accumulate vertical and deep knowledge. Today, contrary to this type of intelligence, the Pop-Up Generation has an 'in-front-of-the-screen' intelligence. It has the ability to switch instantly between two and a half to three dimensions, creating 3D volumes in their minds, as if the popping up of ideas creates shapes and volumes in their brain.

But whereas the deep-thinker has an in-depth and vertical intelligence, possibly with multiple competencies, and aggregates particles of knowledge over months and years, the Pop-Up Generation, based on a zapping and quick-connecting thought process, has a horizontal intelligence that may seem superficial and less deep than the vertical one.

In fact, this horizontal zapping intelligence is a collective intelligence. The particles of knowledge are distributed via various external tools, such as the web, through several brains and social media like Twitter or Facebook, instead of consisting in a single brain. We may think that this distributed collective intelligence reduces the autonomy of the individual, but that is not necessarily so: the more an individual belongs to a network, the more it needs to be autonomous. It is the principle of 'autopoiesis*' in the immune system. Each antibody belongs to an army of antibodies organized in networks, and participates in the construction of that network. In the same way every individual must be open to the outside world to regenerate and contribute to the collectivity.

How the Internet and new technologies affect the brain
The debate on whether a deep intelligence is better

than a zapping collective one is open and it will not be solved here.

What is remarkable to mention, however, is how social media allows mankind to build collective projects and give meaning to emerging phenomena. Take the Jasmine Revolution. Several years ago, the idea of abolishing the establishment was a fleeting thought in the minds of a few people who did not know each other. Through Twitter and Facebook, these people began exchanging thoughts. These thoughts started to aggregate and suddenly, one day, crystallized. The notion of a possible revolution popped up in their brain, and what was once a dream became a reality.

In this reality it appears that humans are no longer solely human. They have become a mix between man and machine, living in a man-machine eco-system, constantly switching from real to virtual worlds, between individual and collective intelligence.

Dr. Martine Naillon holds a PhD in Mathematics and is an expert in Cognitive Sciences and Economic Intelligence. In 2003 she founded Co-Decision Technology in Paris. This company focuses on the patented solution of Co-mining, a technology that allows to model human behavior and to include these findings as a tool for risk analysis.

*Humberto Maturana and Francesco Varela, Autopoiesis and Cognition: The Realization of the Living, Boston Studies in the Philosophy of Science, Cohen, Robert S., and Marx W. Wartofsky, eds, vol 42, Dordrecht, D. Reidel Publishing Co., 1980

MATERIAL DIMENSIONS
Paola Antonelli talks about stretching the boundaries between the tangible and the ephemeral in design practice today.

Tangible vs. Ethics?
Many of the most innovative ideas and concepts in materials today — especially when they come from designers — tend to be ethical. There is a really strong outlook towards the future and an attempt to clean up the foundation of the projects. The design itself can be as hedonistic and as pleasant as possible; it is the source materials and source concept that can be more ethically-biased. I don't see any material that is taboo or any limit to what can be done, except of course the limits of safety.

The first show I did at MoMA was *Mutant Materials in Contemporary Design* (1995). At that time, there was a passing of the baton from chemical engineers and scientists to designers.

Because of new technologies, all of a sudden
we were able to customize materials: it was the
beginning of the era of composites, and there
were much more refined resins that could be
catalyzed at ambient temperatures. The designer
tended to have more human-centered preoccu-
pations, and from here rose the ideas of better
sustainability and a strong ethical awareness.

Moving along the years, I researched software
and even 'wetware', such as the Victimless
Leather and In Vitro Meat, which were featured in *Design in the Elastic Mind* (2008), and
recently with *Talk to Me*, the focus shifted to
the communication between people and objects. The freedom of materials is now so huge
that you might almost say they've stopped being
materials; they have become means and vessels.
You could even consider computer languages
to be materials and processing to be a pleather,
comparable to a basic composite, giving way to
many different expressions.

Possession vs. Immaterial?
In a way, everything can be considered design and where it stops, is more a decision than anything else. For me personally the border lies just before the design of services. I think that there needs to be at least one aspect of design that can be caught by a sense, whether it's scent, sight or tactility. There must be an expression of some sort that can be critical or criticized by people.

I really believe we will need less objects in the future: of course there will always be irresistible things such as shoes and clothing — and we need some degree of superfluosity in life — but I think that there's going to be a distinction between what is superfluous and what is purely pleasure.

Instead, the utilitarian will be more and more about sharing. I really feel that New York City is quite exemplary, for instance, because very few people own cars, yet we are all embracing the use of Zipcars and other forms of temporary use as opposed to the possession of objects.

As the quality of design and technology improves, the world on the computer and the digital world will become more satisfying. I recall the quaint times when virtual reality meant putting on a ridiculous helmet and gloves, but what we have discovered today is that you don't need anything — a computer screen is enough, or even just an iPhone screen — because we tend to dive into spaces if they are really attractive, comfortable or useful. It has nothing to do with Second Life, nor Avatar, nor the virtual reality of helmets and gloves: it's simply inhabiting another space that is an expansion; it's a lateral side-door or window in our physical space. The more this happens, the less that we will need.

Planned obsolescence (companies deliberately manufacturing objects to last a short amount of time) was established in the 1950s and it has recently resurfaced as a scandal and outrage amongst consumers. This reflects ethics and a desire for people to have objects that last longer, such as a dishwasher that lasts for fifteen years. Planned obsolescence was really the anti-apotheosis of consumerism, and to this day, it continues to exist: apparently there are microchips embedded in some of our electronics that make them break at some point, by which repairing them almost outweighs the costs of simply buying a new one.

I am confident that this kind of scandalous behavior will disappear in the future. When you have objects that are more permanent, they have to have last longer, be manufactured better and also be designed better, because if you want to live with them for fifteen years, they have to have an emotional connection and a presence that makes them desirable to be around, enabling them to grow or age with you. It's a very old-fashioned and at the same time, very much a new way of looking at objects. It's very 'European' in the sense that there is more permanence in Europe, as opposed to America and other countries where people have a tendency to be more mobile, from young kids leaving home to study at college to professionals moving around, people often buy a sofa which is left behind when they move on. In Europe, people invest in a sofa maybe once or twice in a lifetime, and the same applies to a dishwasher and so forth.

I appears that children are the educators of their parents when it comes to awareness: asking their parents to pack their sandwiches in recyclable bags, refusing zip-lock bags. To me, the real goal is to make these necessary behavioral changes become normalcy. In order to do so, you need to build the infrastructure: both the education of children and the recycling bins in the street; it goes both ways. Governments and other forms of established and regulated entities need to make it easy for people, and at the same time, people need to educate themselves.

Virtual vs. Technology?

It's inevitable that man will continue to mix with technology. It's how it's been throughout history, only that the technology is different at different times, from steam power to printing and so forth. Technology is not another planet; technology is something that we make, and so it's simply a part of our lives.

Making technology disappear is an important goal. Today, when one wants to see augmented reality, one holds an iPhone up to a barcode in an awkward manner; but maybe one day there will be some other way, using a fan for example — more intuitive, less cumbersome. Technology will always be there and will always be a force, whether benign or malignant, depending on how it is used, and it will be more or less apparent, hopefully because we will be able to modulate it better.

3D printing has captivated our imagination for a long time (it has existed since the 1980s), but the progression in the technology of materials has made it more and more structural. In the beginning, 3D printing was about sculpting foam (something from modeling in architecture and design), before hot resins for making very small objects was introduced. Then the resins got better and one could make bigger objects, before the arrival of stereolithography and all of the different techniques.

What fascinates me is that at some point a choice had to be made. In Belgium, MGX was used by talented designers creating super-elegant objects, but that in the end would cost a lot of money to produce. It was truly a utopian expression of the aesthetic possibilities of the material, and then of course there were all of the geometric and parametric explorations from architectural offices throughout the world.

Now you see that 3D printing has been discovered by the community of hackers, do-it-yourselfers and followers and believers of Make Magazine and all the Maker Faires. This particular community has a sort of Google ethos

— they reject design, almost as if it were an affectation that they want to avoid - but in truth it's like denying God: when you deny design, you affirm it at the same time, so the absence of 'Google' designing is a form of design in itself.

Intriguingly, it's almost as if these hackers discovered 3D printing themselves: although they may make little cups and cupcakes, the difference from before is that it's open source. Previously, with MGX you had to be an established designer or pay a lot of money in order to use the facilities; yet this new movement uses small open source 3D printing machines (such as those distributed by MakerBot Industries @ makerbot. com). Since you can make it yourself, suddenly it's a revolution.

Paola Antonelli is the Senior Curator, Department of Architecture and Design at the Museum of Modern Art, New York

Text from an interview with Philip Fimmano

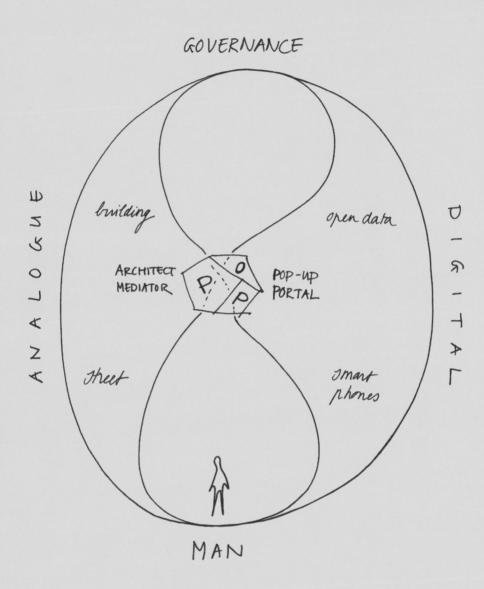

GOVERNANCE

ANALOGUE

DIGITAL

building

open data

ARCHITECT
MEDIATOR

P   O
P

POP-UP
PORTAL

street

smart
phones

MAN

PORTALS TO THE PUBLIC
*Will ephemeral pop-up architecture become the
most solid building artifact of the future city?*
By Hedwig Heinsman

In the warm spring of 2009 a couple of friends
longed for a little holiday retreat close to home.
They decided to take matters into their own hands
and illegally built a tiny summerhouse on a vacant
plot squeezed in between apartment buildings.
They tidied the site, and when the police drove by
they waved ever so politely, as they had no permit.
Curious neighbors, whom they had never talked
to before, were enchanted by the appearance and
asked if they could also use the sandy garden. A
children's birthday party was hosted on the site.
Plants were brought in. The friends made a blog
explaining the house. A grandma brought cookies
and was taught how to read the blog. The next
week she proposed a picnic, on the blog. What
was posted online was brought to the house, and

vice versa. Gardening events, music performances, barbeque restaurants, theatre plays, children's parties, outdoor cinemas, one-day exhibitions, all happened on land that had been vacant until a few weeks before. Then the friends dismantled the building and build it elsewhere in town. But the community remained.

This story is almost true, only the friends were associates in an architecture office. And they realized they had just built a true public building.

Ask a random person about his connection to the 'public domain' and he's likely to return it with a puzzled comment about the web. In the mean time, the amount of 'public buildings'— community centers, schools, libraries, museums, the lot — is reducing. And while digital connectivity rises, we more and more disconnect from the physical streets. The term 'architect' might as well refer to a software engineer. This intermediary notion of 'online and offline' on all kinds of societal levels portrays an intriguing parallel with the changing role of the architect. Global and local societies are more than ever in a transient, interconnected and complex twilight in-between state. This brings up the question whether the architect should not adapt to a more fluid attitude, riding the waves of the city's tidal changes instead of obstructing it with long-due buildings. In Western extant city layouts with a surplus of heritage heavy and vacant buildings, the question arises how to play the existing urban context, instead of planning it. Architecture becomes as much about mobile activities as building, and the architect becomes a curator, reprogramming spaces and bringing people together within temporary settings. And this is where the architectural pop-up pops up.

Through the pop-up*, the role of the architect and the relation to his building, however ephemeral, come together. It could perhaps be drawn up best by a Vitruvian-man like scheme of perfect proportion, where the man in the middle once again connects all elements and parties involved in the process directly around him within his self-constructed environment. With help of the pop-up, designers could, in the words of John Thackara, "evolve from being the individual authors of objects or buildings, to being the facilitators of change among large groups of people."[1] The pop-up is the template for change, and the location where the architect mediates.

The pop-up has several crucial characteristics that share the ability to make an immediate and catalyzing impact onto their surroundings. All pop-ups share a sense of 'adhocism' — a term coined by Charles Jencks, who states: "a purpose immediately fulfilled is the ideal of adhocism; it cuts through the usual delays caused by specialization, bureaucracy and hierarchical organization" [2]. Pop-ups are simply suddenly there. They are abrupt, urgent, and demand instant response and interference. And while these characteristics in the virtual world ('damn these pop-up adds why is the pop-up blocker not working') ignite a mere frustrated mouse click, in the real world they have a much more positive effect. Built pop-ups instigate human motion. And as such, they work as a built interface. A means to let the 'public' act again and intervene and retake the streets.

This notion of a built interface becomes more multi-faceted when seen in relation to the Internet. When connected to the simplest blog or representation of sorts online, pop-ups can link the analogue and the digital domain, and become true public portals from the real into the virtual and vice versa. Suddenly the pop-up building becomes an elemental Heideggers' Hut 3.0, instantly linking virtual thought to location. They are a means to connect small local objects with a large global audience. In a similar way, the pop-up also becomes a portal between top-down and bottom-up. Governmental authorities can use them as a means to directly (re)connect with their audience. And in their turn, local, also non-digitally connected, citizens can be educated

and make their ideas public, both real and online.
The pop-up is a flexible filter to let urban ideas
trickle up. Now the traditional categories of
capitalist, government, right and left become
more dispersed, future policies will increasingly
become more about direct interference with the
public. 'Guerrilla advertisement' is already
becoming a commodity and this puts the concept
of guerrilla government in a new perspective,
especially when seen in the light of growing
access to open data and open source culture.
Here, in their ability to create an instant place and
platform, pop-ups can portray a new democratic
architecture. At the pop-up platform people can
post and comment, akin the traditional Swiss
Landsgemeinde ('cantonal assembly') as a place of
direct democracy, where every villager could
interrupt and react. Mind you, we're not talking
total self-organizing groups and systems here. This
new type of physical Facebook does shape the way
its visitors organize themselves: the design of the
built interface co-curates the public agenda.

Varying from fully equipped amphibian architecture to haphazard haystacks, the design of the pop-up is of great importance. And although their look and feel may differ, what unites them is their ad-hoc quality to add-on. All pop-ups add to the existing context, instead of entirely demolishing what was before. They give new meaning to sites, and in their often-makeshift character, also to unusual materials. This re-use and re-interpretation of site and material on several scale levels makes the pop-up very sustainable and introduces a new kind of urban vernacular: people can read the sum of the signs of time, recognize and understand its parts and traces, and therefore are likely to appreciate what they see. Plus, because of this rooted understanding, they are more likely not to be afraid to join in and build along. Pop-ups can create social value by mixing up seemingly worthless things, or in other words, create more with less.

Thinking in terms of property development, this ability to generate value at limited investment also makes the pop-up a profitable portal to growth, and even to permanent buildings. Pop-up architecture can play a durable and integral role in city development — not just as a mere provisional strategy in terms of crisis — as part of a city-script: Here pop-ups are build to grow and perhaps flourish to become permanent buildings, or simply vanish again. On a local level within the script, private homeowners could tweak and transform their homes by attaching permanent pop-ups to their houses, when they are in need for more or different space. This has a constructive price-quality ratio, but also allows for the users to literally and figuratively be more attached to their home and location.

Thus, pop-ups by all means make architecture again something of the present. Startlingly enough, thereby they also become a portal to the future. In the digital domain, the term 'beta-testing' is widely known. In the same way, pop-up building serves as a perfect means to test utopian projects for real in beta-mode. The community can respond at an early stage, bring input and thereby optimize the project whilst it simultaneously already has a positive effect on the community, and its own social/economic value. This 'betapreneurial' double feedback loop can be instigated by all kinds of unsolicited programmatic building proposals, as a kind of entrepreneurial research-in-reverse. Some projects will kick-start from snowball to avalanche; others might melt like mental monuments. But, as also one-day-events can have eternal worth in the collective memory of the visitors, a public city needs these momentary monuments. And suddenly so, pop-up architecture, the most ephemeral of sorts, could actually be the most solid building artifact of the future city.

pop-up architecture should not be confused with pop-up book papercraft architecture. 'Pop-in' would probably be the exact word here, a combination of pop-up (to appear) and plug-in (to attach).

[1] Thackara, The MIT Press (2005) In the Bubble: Designing in a Complex World
[2] Jencks, C. and Silver, N. (1972) Adhocism, the case for Improvisation, Aricula Press, Inc.

Hedwig Heinsman co-founded DUS architects in 2004 together with Hans Vermeulen and Martine de Wit. DUS builds 'public architecture': Architecture that influences the public domain using scale 1:1 models, urban process design and strategy design, and that ranges from temporary interiors to long-term urban transformation trajectories.

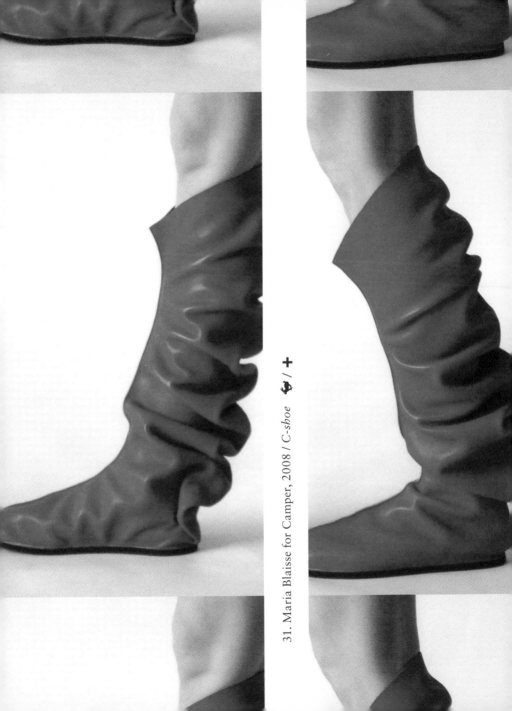

31. Maria Blaisse for Camper, 2008 / *C-shoe* 🐾 / +

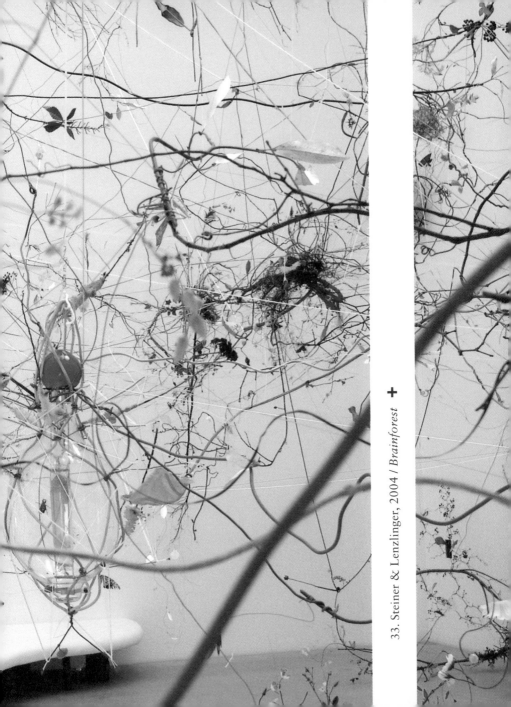

33. Steiner & Lenzlinger, 2004 / *Brainforest* +

33. Steiner & Lenzlinger, 2005 / Zimmerpflanzen und Schweinefutter +

34. Yuko Takada Keller, 2011 / *Prismatic* 😊 / +

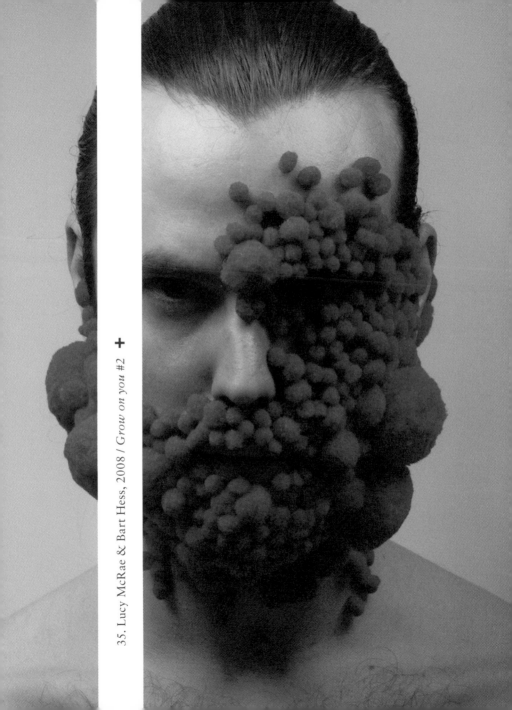

35. Lucy McRae & Bart Hess, 2008 / *Grow on you #2*

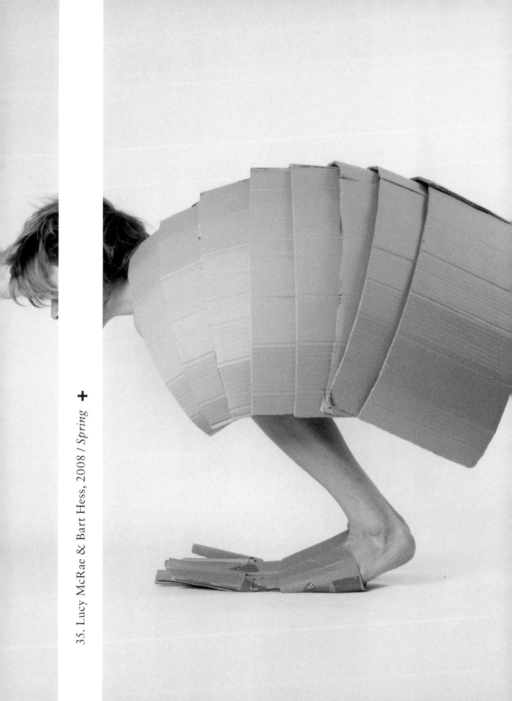

35. Lucy McRae & Bart Hess, 2008 / *Spring* +

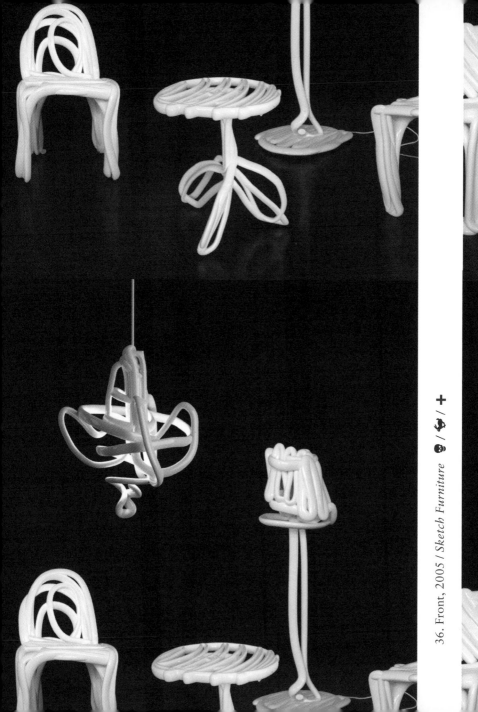

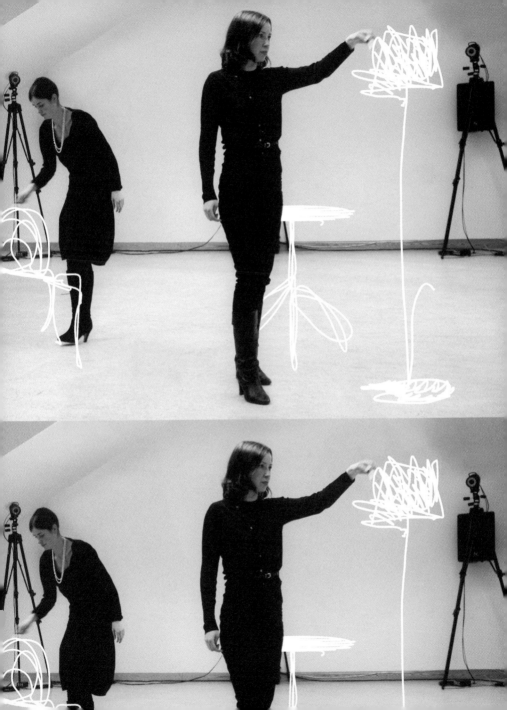

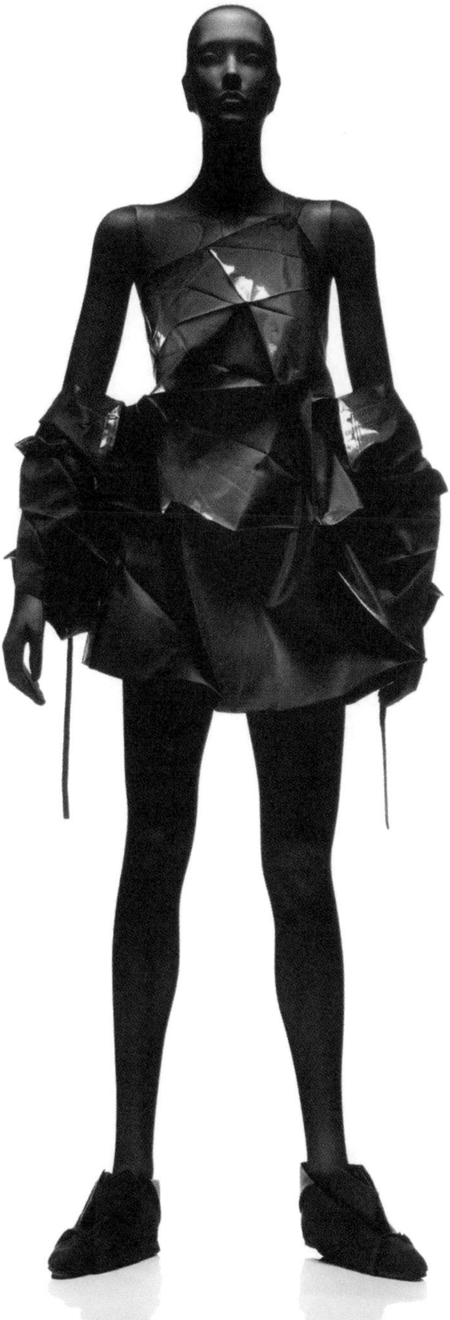

37. Issey Miyake, 2010 / 132.5 + /

38. Carolina Wilcke, 2009 / *Kamerrekwisiet* ☻ / ✚

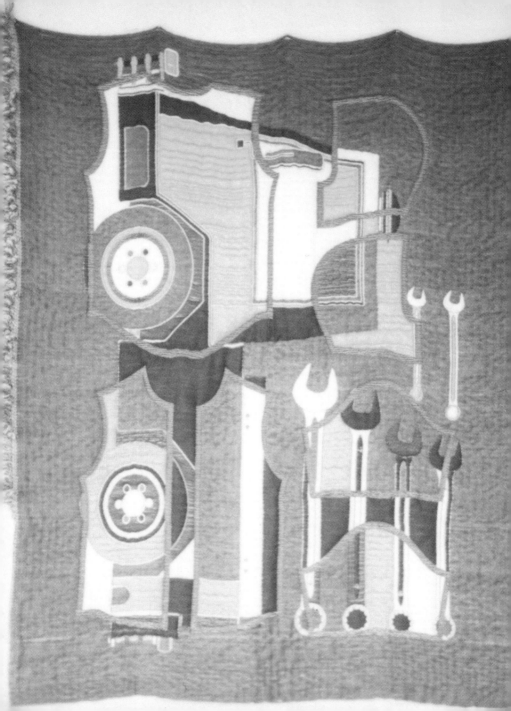

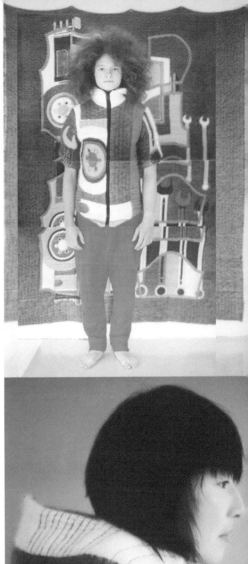

39. Borre Akkersdijk, 2010 / *Ready Made*
supported by Audax Textielmuseum Tilburg / TextielLab   *Photo credit: Marie Taillefer*

🐏 / 🎨 / +

40. Molo, 2008 / *Fanning Stool, Softseating* 👁 / 🐒 / + / 🗼

41. Yochai Matos, 2011 / *Landscape* 😊 / ✚

42. Anthony Kleinepier, 2008 / *Evergreen, Grass Room Divider* 🐸 / +

43. Thomas Raschke, 2000 / *Wire Frames, Musik* ✛ / 🪕

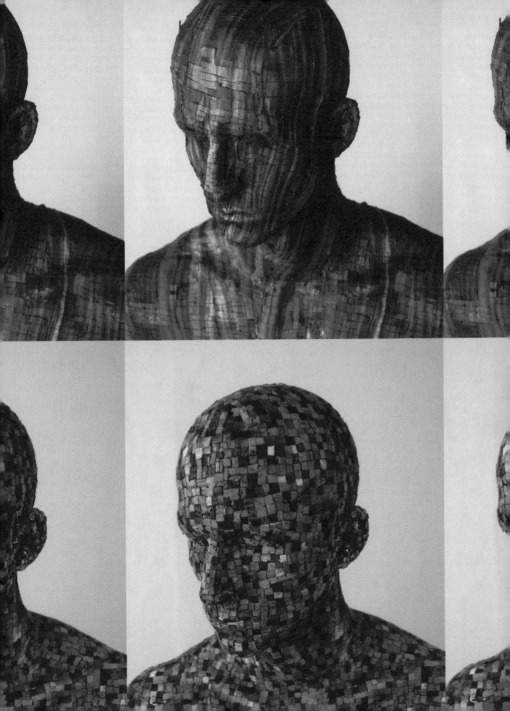

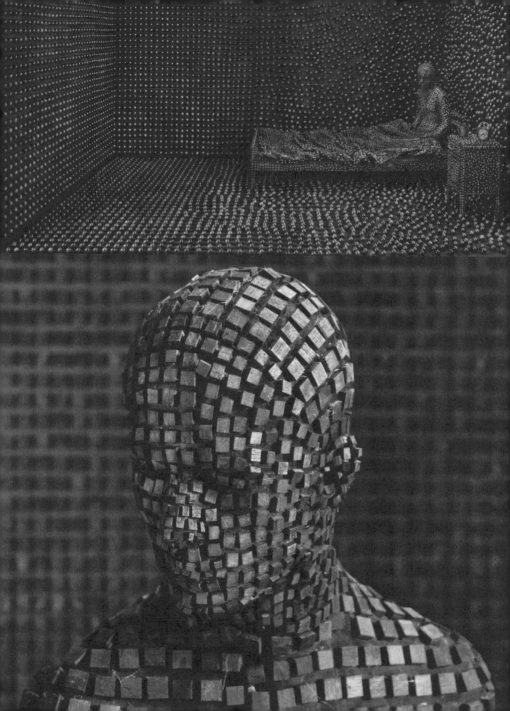

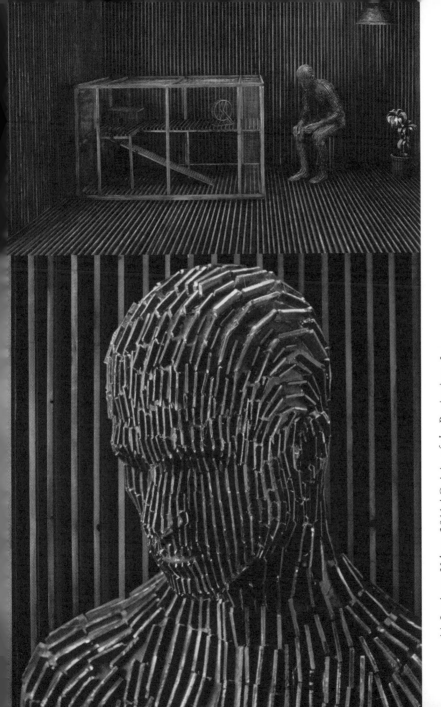

44. Levi van Veluw, 2011 / *Origin of the Beginning* +

45. Camille Scherrer, 2008 / *Le Monde des Montagnes* + / 🏃

46. Studio Makkink & Bey/SV Prooff, 2009 / Prooff furniture 🐑 / + / 🏃 *Photo credit: Stijn Brakkee*

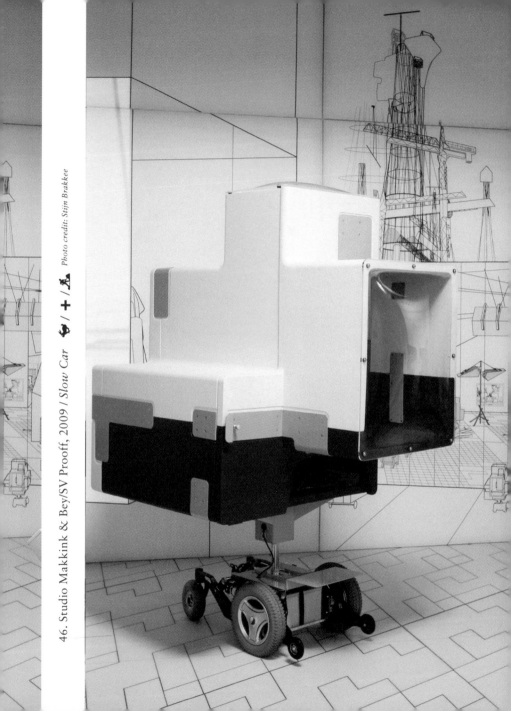

46. Studio Makkink & Bey/SV Prooff, 2009 / *Slow Car* 🐌 / + / 🏃 *Photo credit: Stijn Brakkee*

47. L/B, 2011 / Beautiful Bridge #1 🌐 / ✦

48. Jacob Dahlgren, 2011 / *Demonstration August 16 – Playing the City*  *Photo credit: Cem Yücetas*

49. Suzanne Oxenaar, 2011 / *Llove Hotel* ☻ / 🐟 / ✚

50. Chris Bosse, 2007 / *Digital Origami* 🐸 / +

51. DUS Architects, 2010 / *Bucky Bar* ☕ / 🦞 / 🔥

52. Lambert Kamps, 2007 / *Caterpillar* 😈 / 🐛 / ⚰

53. Studio Tord Boontje for Habitat, 2002 & Artecnica, 2004 / *Garland* 🐾 / + / ⚘

54. Atelier Pariri, 2011 / *Is it still Type?* ✝ / 🔥

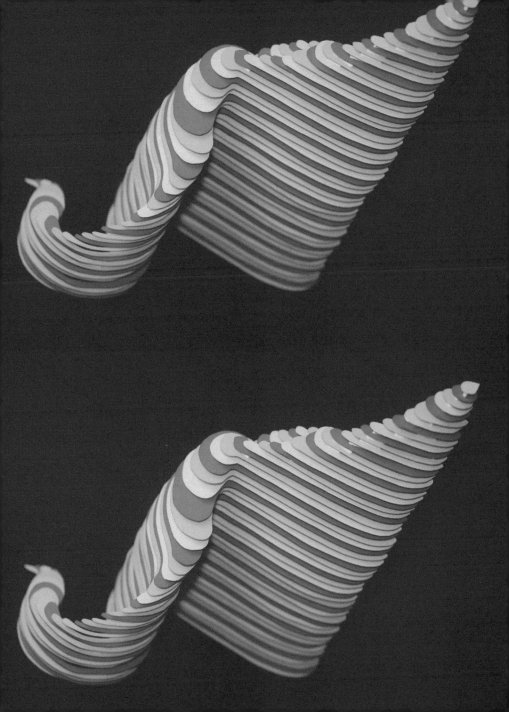

54. Atelier Pariri, 2011 / *Space Typo* + / 🦋

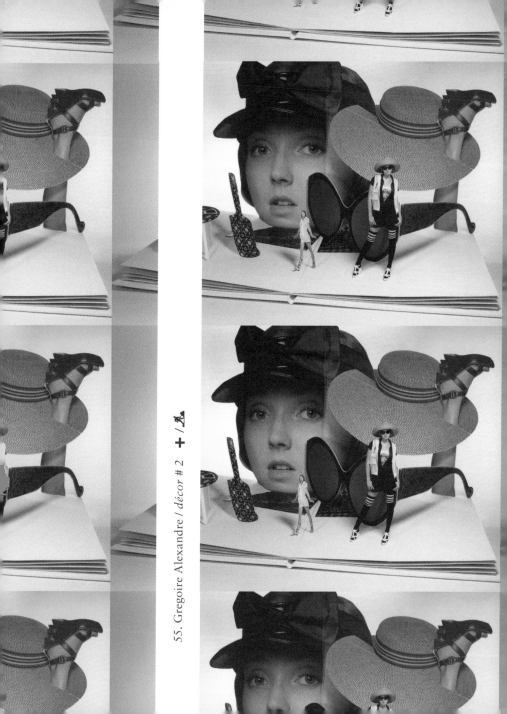

55. Gregoire Alexandre / *décor # 2* ✝ / 🐑

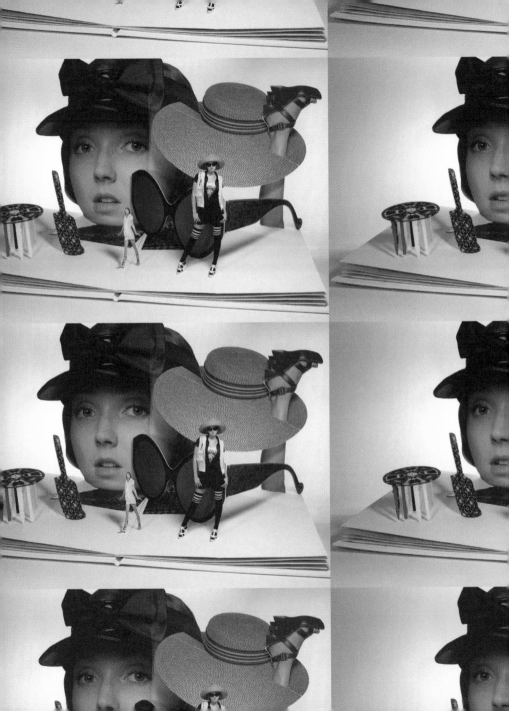

56. Christian Tagliavini, 2008 / *Cubism III, Dame di Cartone Series* ✚

56. Christian Tagliavini, 2008 / 17th Century II, Dame di Cartone Series +

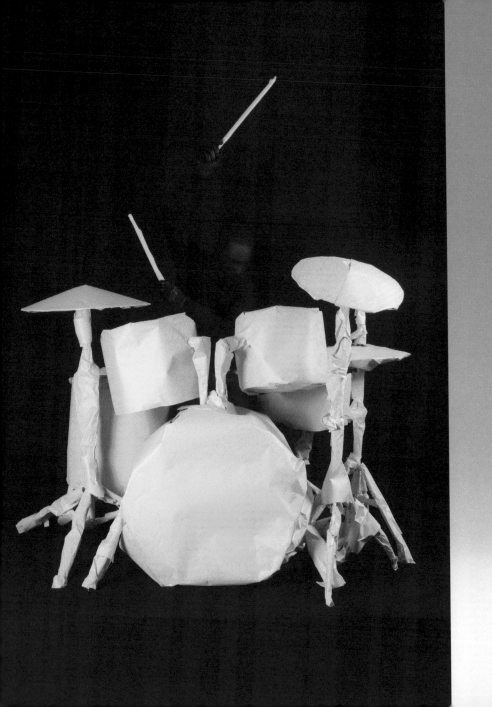

57. Akatre, 2010 / Mood 21,25,18 ✚ / 🏔

58. Carmela Bogman & Rogier Martens, 2010 / *Pop-up Street Furniture* 🌐 / 🐸 / +

60. Softlab, 2009 / *pAlice Installation* +

61. Abigail Reynolds / *Big Ben and Thames 61 82* 🌓 / +

1. THE ROYAL HOSPITAL, GREENWICH. This noble group of Thames-side buildings, now the home of the National Maritime Museum and the Royal Naval War College, was begun by Charles II and completed to the designs of Sir Christopher Wren in the reign of William III.

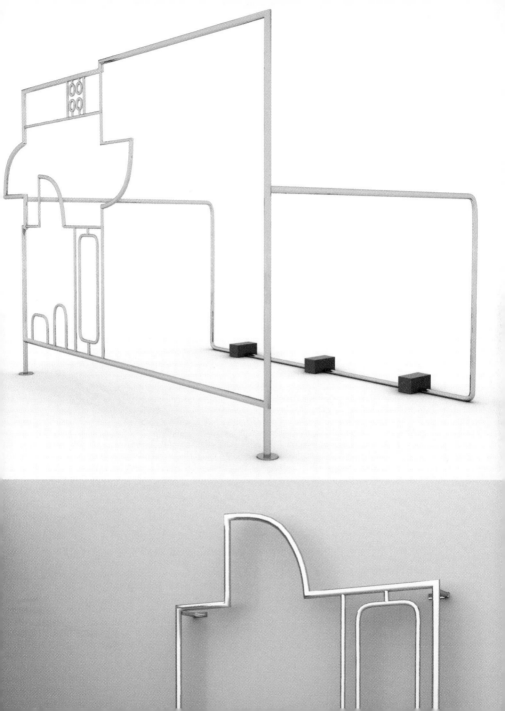

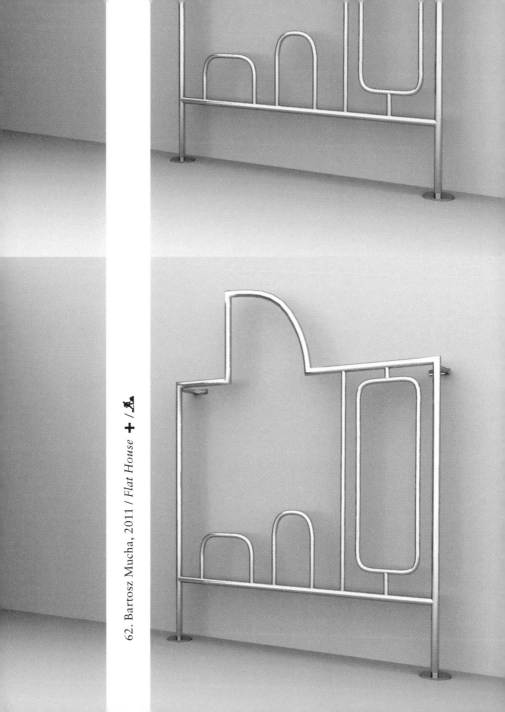

62. Bartosz Mucha, 2011 / *Flat House* ✚ / 🏃

63. Tonkin Liu, 2006 / *Swinging Ringing Tree* 🎭 / 🐾 / +

Photo credit: John Lyons 1,2,3 on behalf of Burnley Borough Council

64. Brigitte Kowanz, 2007 / *Moments* 😊 / +

65. Electroland, 2004 / Urban Nomad Shelter 👾 / 🐦 / + / ♿

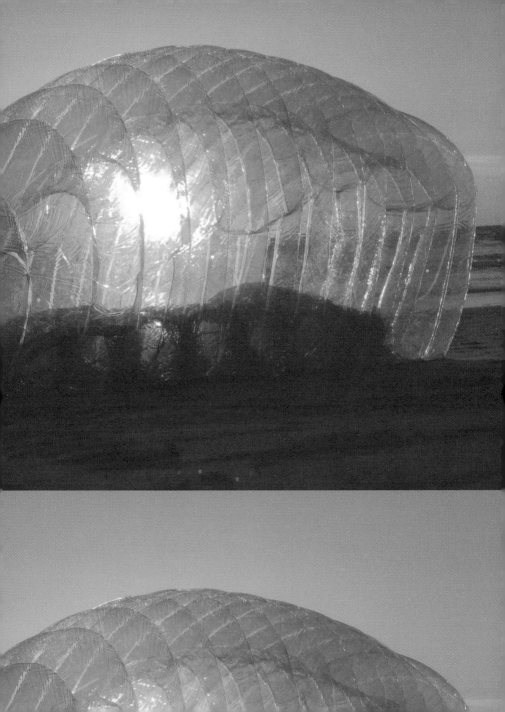

66. André Chénier, 2011 / *Bregenzer Festspiele* / Karl Forste +

67. Torafu Architects, 2011 / *Light Loom* for Canon, Salone Internazionale del Mobile ● / ✦ / ✛

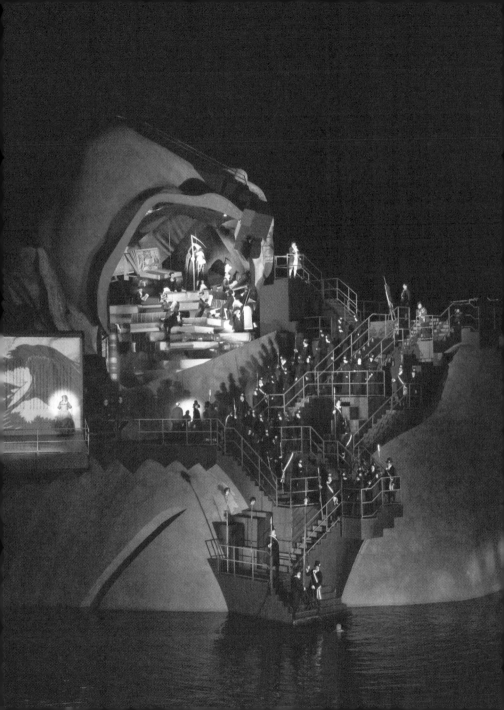

INDEX

CREDITS

This publication was published on the occasion
of the exhibition *The Pop-Up Generation: Design
Between Dimensions*, curated by Lidewij Edelkoort
(MOTI, Breda: December 11, 2011 – April 16,
2012, to be followed by a European tour in 2012–
2013). The exhibition features the work of the
following artists and designers, and came about in
collaboration with several regional industries from
the Dutch province of Noord-Brabant, to all of
whom we are most grateful.

Designers:
Borre Akkersdijk
BCXSY
Tord Boontje
Catharina van Eetvelde
Kiki van Eijk
Eley Kishimoto & Ben Wilson
Carla Fernández
Front

Anna Garforth
Jaime Hayon
Niels Hoebers
Anthony Kleinepier
Eric Ku
Laurens Manders
Niels Meulman
Issey Miyake
Molo
Bartosz Mucha
Camille Scherrer
Rodrigo Solórzano
Studio Job
Carolina Wilcke
Richard Woods & Sebastian Wrong

Collaborators:
Audax Textiel Museum, Textiel Lab
Concorp B.V.
Desso B.V.
Geton Roestvrijstaalindustrie B.V.
John Vos meubelatelier